Wykonanie 12 Kompanii Geograficznej 2 Korpusu
Italia 1944

'54 pkt. 550

❶ Monte Oro	❻ D'Onofrio Ridge	⓫ Monte Castellone
❷ Hangman's Hill	❼ Point 569	⓬ Point 893
❸ Cassino town	❽ Point 593 (Monte Calvario)	⓭ Point 912
❹ Point 193 (Rocca Janula)	❾ Phantom Ridge	⓮ Monte Cairo
❺ The Abbey	❿ Point 706	

CASSINO

Anatomy of the battle

CASSINO

Anatomy of the battle

Janusz Piekalkiewicz

Title page: An 8th Army soldier looks across the valley of the river Gari in May 1944 as a smokescreen drifts down to cover the Bailey bridge across the river.

Acknowledgements

The author would like to thank the following individuals who have been most helpful: Herr Dr. M. Haupt; Herr M. Nilges, Herr W. Held, B.A. Koblenz; Frau Dr. M. Lindemann, Frau H. Rajkovik, I.f.Z. Dortmund; Herr W. Haupt, B.f.Z. Stuttgart; Herr J. Ortstein, Frau B. Wohlan, ZB.d. Bw. Dusseldorf; Brig-Gen. I. Bardon, Bonn; Brig-Gen. R. B. C. Plowden, Bonn; Col. A. Viviani, Bonn; Frau I. Kopf, US Library Bonn; Herr Dr. F. G. Maier, Bern; Mr. J. S. Lucas, Mr. P. H. Reed, I.W.M. London; the staff of the Photographic Library, I.W.M. London; Capt. R. Dembinski, curator of the Sikorski Institute, London; Capt. W. Milewski, London; Capt. St. Zurakowski, London; Mrs. R. Oppman, London; Ing. K. Barbarski, London; Col. Dr. M. Motek, London; Col. W. D. Kasprowicz, London; Mr. P. Roland, E.C.E.P.D.A. Paris; Capt. C. L. Blische, Washington, D.C.; Mrs. M. B. Livesay, Arlington; Mr. W. H. Leary, N.A. Washington D.C.; Herr Dr. D. Bradley, Munster; Herr K. Kirchner, Erlangen; Col. a. D. H. A. Koch, Bonn; Frau H. Muller, Rosrath; Herr A. Tanzer, Dusseldorf; Herr Dr. J. Kohler, Gustav Lubbe Verlag, Bergisch Gladbach, and Herr F. Forder, Bergisch Gladbach.

There are three individuals whose help was particularly invaluable: Col. (Bw) a.D. Dr. C. H. Hermann, Rheinbach; Maj. R. L. Walton, London, and Capt. B. D. Samuelson, Washington. D.C.

Picture Sources: Bundesarchiv Koblenz; Etablissement Cinématographique et Photographique des Armées, Fort d'Ivry; Imperial War Museum, London; National Archives, Washington, D.C.; US Air Force, Arlington, Virginia; US Army, Washington, D.C.; Sikorsky Institute, London; M.R. de Launay Library, Paris; A. Stilles Library, New York; Klaus Kirchner, Verlag fur zeitgenossische Dokumente und Curiosa, Erlangen; Robert Hunt Library; Archiv J. Piekalkiewicz.

Apart from the official communiques and messages issued by the high command of each side, the commentaries on the development of the campaign were quoted from the following sources: *The Times*, London; Radio Beromünster, Switzerland; the German newspaper *Völkischer Beobachter* (directly controlled by Goebbels); the German News Bureau; the International Information Bureau (a branch of the German News Bureau); SS reports, and Stefani's Agency (an Italian fascist news agency).

ISBN 0-85613-021-4

First US Edition published by Historical Times, Inc., Harrisburg, PA 17105
Published in 1988.

ISBN 0-918678-32-3

Library of Congress Cataloging-in-Publication Data
Piekalkiewicz, Janusz.
Battle for Cassino
Cassino: anatomy of the battle/Janusz Piekalkiewicz. – 1st US ed.
American ed. published under title: The battle for Cassino.
Reprint. Originally published: London: Orbis, © 1980.
Bibliography: p.
Includes index.
ISBN 0-918678-32-3
1. Cassino (Italy), Battle of, 1944. I. Title.
D763. I82C266 1987 940.54′21 – dc19 87-32303

Printed by Kingsport Press, Kingsport, TN 37662
Manufactured in the United States of America

CONTENTS

THE SETTING

DURING THE SUMMER of 1943 the war slowly approached Italy, one of the great historical centres of western culture.

The boot-shaped peninsula is about 1600km (1000 miles) long and up to 160km (100 miles) wide; the backbone of the Abruzzi mountains extends for almost the whole length with individual ranges up to 2000m (6600 feet) high. On the eastern side the mountains stretch like ribs to the Adriatic coast. On the western side, towards the Tyrrhenian Sea, the heights at first lie almost parallel to the Abruzzi mountains, then fade away to the south.

Allied operations in 1943–4 took in both coastal sectors: an Adriatic front about 8–24km (5–15 miles) in width and a western front, on the Tyrrhenian Sea, 32–40km (20–25 miles) wide. Divided by the impassable mountain massif, they formed two almost separate theatres of war. The greatest problem was communication: the few roads in the interior were tortuous, narrow and in winter scarcely negotiable.

Rome and Naples are joined by two roads, the famous Via Appia, also known as Highway 7, which runs from the west coast over the Pontine Marshes to the Eternal City, and Highway 6, the old Via Casilina. The Roman legions of Fabius once assembled along it to oppose Hannibal, and in the 6th century AD the Via Casilina was used by the Byzantine general, Belisarius, to wrest the Eternal City from the Goths, who themselves were led along the road to battle.

Between Naples and Rome stretch mountain ridges difficult to climb, and extremely precipitous on their southern and south-eastern slopes. The landscape here is distinctly alpine in character, and, in addition, both on the Adriatic and on the Tyrrhenian Sea, the mountains could only be negotiated using narrow strips of land which in places were marshy as well.

Opposite: Dominating the landscape around, the great Benedictine Abbey of Monte Cassino in the summer of 1943.

In the interior the only suitable route for motorized units making for Rome was along the 10km (6 miles) wide Liri valley, the entrance to which is dominated by the rocky promontory crowned by Monte Cassino. The lowest knoll here is 300m (1000 feet) high, and the highest, the massif of Monte Cairo, the summit of which is covered in snow almost all year round, rises to about 1700m (5500 feet). The hills, which would gain a dolorous fame by being named again and again in the military communiqués, are so arranged that the top of each looks out over its neighbours and supporting fire could be directed from one to another.

South of Cassino, near Monte Trocchio, the Via Casilina leaves the mountains and enters the Rapido valley. After running dead straight for 5km (3 miles) it makes a sharp turn to the south and goes round Monte Cassino in the direction of the Liri valley. At the foot of Monte Cassino on the northern edge of the town rises Rocca Janula, a rock about 90m (300 feet) high, surmounted by a ruined castle. A saddle of rock joins Monte Cassino and Rocca Janula: this was the most direct, though the hardest, path to the abbey.

During the classical period, there was a temple to Apollo on the 516m (1700 feet) high Monte Cassino. It belonged to the Acropolis, the citadel of ancient Casinum, a wealthy Roman town.

In AD 524, St. Benedict erected the first properly organized monastery in Italy, a church with a refugium for his small community of monks, on the ruins of the temple. Benedict of Nursia was born in about 480, the son of a wealthy landowner in the province of Perugia. He was a quiet, shy man who after a short period of study retreated from the world 'to be nearer to God'. For a long time he lived in a cave above Subiaco near Rome. Here he gathered disciples around him and here arose the original form of the monastic community. For the first time, in his later famous 'Benedictine Rule', he gave a group of monks firm, practical, wise and clearly formulated regulations governing their order. In 547, he died on Monte Cassino aged about sixty-five. The abbey he founded became the birthplace of monasticism and for many centuries was one of the spiritual centres of the West. The rule of the monastic community prescribed strict alternating periods of work and prayer; the Benedictines worked as missionaries, scholars and educators and profoundly influenced the spirit of the Middle Ages.

In 569 the Lombards invaded Italy, and Monte Cassino fell victim to their onslaught. The monks escaped to Rome, saving the original text of the 'Benedictine Rule', but the monastery of Monte Cassino was not re-built until 717, by Pope Gregory II. The Benedictine Order now came out of its isolation and founded educational establishments and hospitals. In 778 Charlemagne visited the monastery and made the Benedictines the foremost order in the Frankish Empire. The Abbot of Monte Cassino became Lord High Chancellor of the Empire and was personally responsible to the Emperor.

The Saracens plundered the monastery and set it on fire in 883. It was rebuilt in 20 years, and, although it was destroyed by the Normans in 1030, for the rest of the 11th century Monte Cassino experienced a golden age, under the greatly respected Abbot Desiderius, later Pope Victor III. In the re-built abbey he founded a school for painting miniatures famous throughout Europe, and also built a monastery church richly decorated with mosaics and frescoes. As the Benedictines were not averse to worldly pleasures, however, Pope Celestine V placed the abbey under the control of the Celestine Order in 1294, owing to the 'continuous disorder in the life of the monks'. Pope Boniface VIII repealed the directive, and under Pope John XXII the abbey was declared a bishopric in the early 14th century.

On 9 September 1349 a powerful earthquake almost completely destroyed the monastery. Re-building was begun at once, particularly encouraged by Pope Urban V who appointed himself abbot in 1367. He also laid down that all Benedictine abbeys had to pay a tax for the re-building of the parent monastery.

The monastery was based around five courtyards, and was a vast complex of buildings. From below, it looked like a fortress; in spite of being built of light-coloured stone, the grim rows of cell windows, crenellation, and long walls belied its religious intent. The main features of the monastery designed by Pope Urban V were preserved until 15 February 1944.

In 1504 Monte Cassino was united with 95 abbeys and 100 monasteries to form a system of estates. From that time the abbot bore the title of 'Head of all Abbots of the Benedictine Order, Chancellor and Grand Chaplain of the Roman Empire, Prince of Peace'.

During the Renaissance the monastery became a favourite place of pilgrimage and a centre for fine arts. 'In 1600 more than 100 pilgrims lingered daily at Monte Cassino, and the Benedictines, true to their Rule, washed their feet and served them at table,' noted the chroniclers. Torquato Tasso, one of the greatest Italian poets, also found refuge here. In 1625 alone there were 80,000 visitors.

The Benedictines were constantly at pains to render their abbey even more beautiful. In 1613, Orazio Torrianis from Mendrisio built a magnificent cupola for the monastery church. The rich stucco work in the sacristy was created by Simonetti, another Ticino master from Astano. Then, in the 18th century, several generations of the best artists in Italy worked on the splendid church which became a baroque show-piece.

In May 1799 the monastery was plundered by the French under General Olivier, but after 1815 it was restored to its former status.

In 1868, like all other monasteries in Italy, the abbey lost its possessions to the new Italian kingdom; the abbey itself became state property and was declared a national monument. Only the right of use was left to the Benedictine fathers. The library of the abbey remained, however, one of the most important in the world, containing as it did 2000 codices decorated with miniatures, 40,000 manuscripts and 250 incunabulae, amongst them works such as Varro's *De Lingua Latina* , (the oldest extant grammatical work) and much of the writings of Tacitus, Cicero, Horace, Ovid, Virgil, Seneca and many others.

Cassino, situated halfway between Naples and Rome and known as St. Germano until 1871, was, in 1939, a typical Abruzzi town with four churches, four hotels, a prison and a small railway station. Together with the small villages nearby it numbered about 22,000 inhabitants and had a built-up area of about 64 hectares (160 acres). As almost everywhere in Italy, the buildings were constructed of solid stone.

Cassino was already known in the 4th century BC under the name of Casinum. Apart from a villa belonging to Mark Antony, the usual aqueducts, temples and a large amphitheatre, there were also Roman thermal baths, which were in use up to the Second World War.

In the valley were rows of fruitful orchards and fields; olive-groves and vineyards shared the lower slopes with thick woods of oak, spruce and acacia. The Rapido, which had its source in the north of the Abruzzi, wound through the outskirts of Cassino and after joining the Cesa Martino was known as the Gari. Further south the Gari met the Liri which flowed from the west, and became the Garigliano. The surrounding mountains were covered with thorn bushes, the only vegetation able to withstand the stormy wind and the burning sun.

Italy was a land ideal for defence. As soon as one mountain or river barrier was overcome the next one was already blocking the way. Again, the few level areas were too small to allow the Allies to make decisive use of their armoured forces. The Germans were past masters of the rules of defensive delaying tactics: in a position to be given up one group of soldiers would remain behind for a few hours as rearguards, another group would withdraw early and occupy a second line nearby, and a third group would be detailed as advance post for this new position. In this way the retreat gained elasticity, depth and strength. A platoon with a single machine-gun was often able to hold a favourable position for hours, gaining valuable time.

On the advice of Field-Marshal Kesselring, Commander-in-Chief of Army Group C, Hitler had altered his strategy in Italy in 1943. Originally, on the recommendations of Field-Marshal Rommel, he had intended to pull back his forces behind Rome and to construct a strong front line in northern Italy. Now he ordered that the Allies were to be resisted fiercely at a point as far south as possible.

The decision to defend Cassino had thus already been taken when the US 5th Army (Lt.-General Clark) was still almost 100km (60 miles) away. The 'waist' of Italy, the narrowest point on the peninsula, between the Gulf of Gaeta in the west and the mouth of the Sangro in the east, offered the most favourable sector for defensive fighting. It was also crucial to gain enough time for the planned construction of extensive defensive positions. Here, delaying tactics would give way to rigid defence.

It was decided to build three parallel lines slanting across the peninsula 12–18km (7–11 miles) apart. The Reinhard Line, also known to the Allies as the Winter Line, ran from the mouth of the Garigliano in the west, over the Abruzzi and along the Sangro to the Adriatic coast. This line, which was only a chain of light field-works, was a sort of forward position occupied by the German troops streaming back from southern Italy. Behind it, running along the

Italian prisoners at work on the Gustav Line under the supervision of their German captors. The natural strength of the position is shown by the valley stretching away below.

course of the Rapido, the Gari and the Garigliano, the next position, the Gustav Line, was constructed. This position consisted of a row of fortress-like strong points, some of them concrete, in the valley bottom behind the rivers and along ridge positions in the high mountains which were perfect for defence. Owing to the nature of the ground the deep defensive zone, several kilometres wide, was immensely strong. The monastery of Monte Cassino lay in this line of defence.

The inhabitants of the town of Cassino were evacuated and numerous houses were further reinforced by the addition of fortified

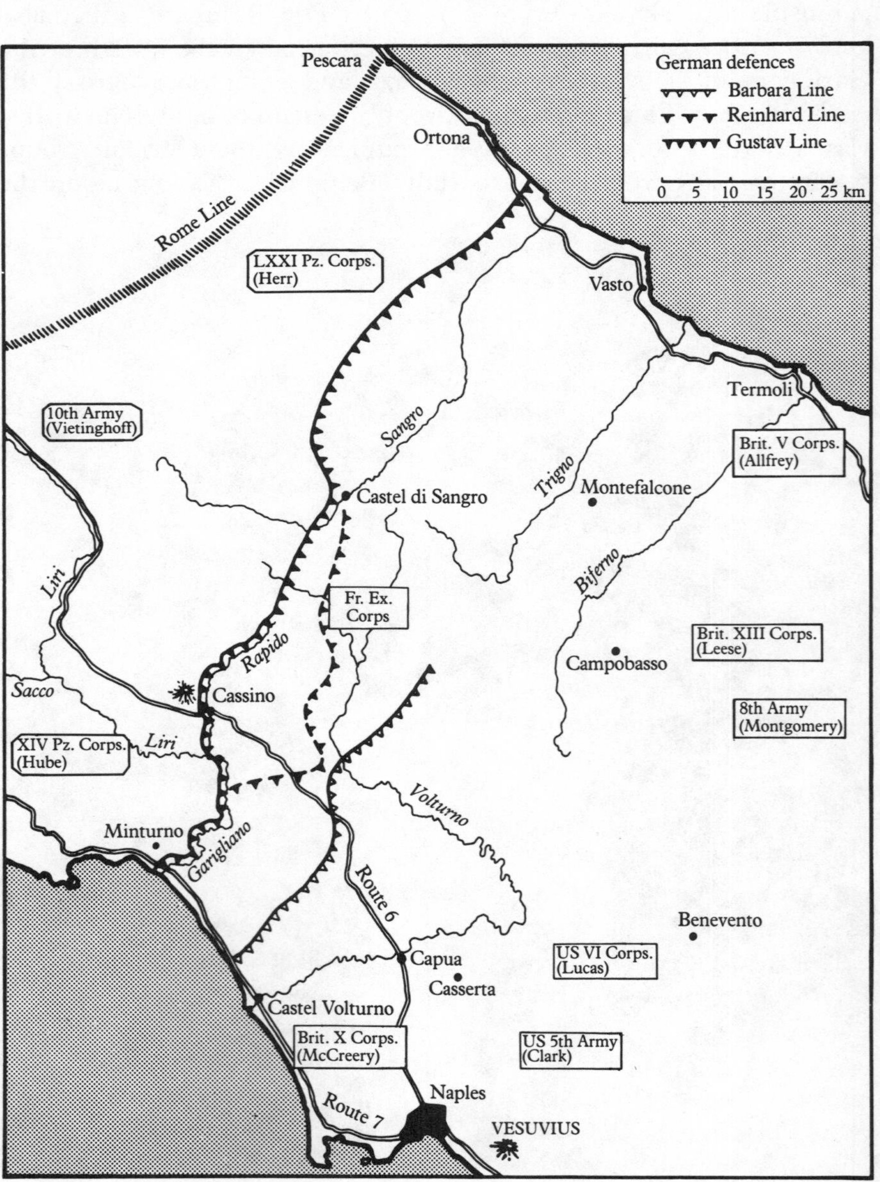

The German defence lines confronting the Allies.

Troops of the French Expeditionary Corps look across the mountains which dominated the battle and dictated the tactics and manoeuvres of both sides.

shelters or bunkers. In some of the larger buildings which had a good field of fire tanks were positioned. In the northern part of the town the Rapido was dammed, so that in heavy rain the Liri valley could be flooded. A crucial factor in the defence of the Cassino sector was the excellent potential for observation, which allowed the Germans to exploit the fortifications and make full use of troops and equipment.

The third and last line of fortification between Cassino and Rome was the *Senger-Riegel*, named after Lt.-General von Senger und Etterlin; it was also known as the Hitler Line. In the event of a breakthrough this line was to form a connection from Terracina to the northern wing of the Gustav Line and serve as a second position. The *Senger-Riegel* was partly fortified with concrete shelters and 10m (33 feet) wide tank traps.

Owing to the difficult terrain the strong Allied armoured forces were almost exclusively confined to the roads, which suited the German anti-tank defence very well. Nature had ensured that the initiative and the advantage of surprise in this theatre of war constantly lay with the defenders; and in the coming winter they expected that nature would help them even more, with mud in the valleys and heavy snowfalls in the mountains.

The Germans had enough time to prepare the defence of Cassino and they took full advantage of it. It took four bloody offensives over a period of almost six months before the Allies broke through the deep defensive zone at Cassino and fought their way to Rome.

DRAMATIS PERSONAE

Harold Alexander

Opposite: Harold Alexander

Commander-in-Chief Allied Forces in Italy, soldier through and through, a cultivated man with a deeply sympathetic imagination and a skilled diplomat, Alexander commanded probably the most international fighting forces of the Second World War: Americans, British, French, Italians, New Zealanders, Canadians, South Africans, Indians, Brazilians, Jews and Poles.

Harold Alexander was born in London on 10 December 1891. After education at Harrow and Sandhurst he joined the Irish Guards in 1911. During the First World War he led a battalion in France, was wounded three times and received a number of decorations. In March 1919 he served with the Allied Military Mission in Warsaw, and in the same year commanded the Baltic militia against the Red Army. Between the wars he held several commands, including one on the North-West Frontier of India.

On the outbreak of the Second World War, he became commander of the 1st Division of the British Expeditionary Force under General Lord Gort in France. Then, after his return to England on 31 May 1940 as commanding general of 1 Corps, Alexander played a major part in the successful evacuation of British troops from Dunkirk.

From June 1940 he was in charge of Southern Command, the most important area for defence against the expected German invasion. One of his major contributions was the introduction of unorthodox training and fighting methods into the British Army. After the danger of a German landing was past, Alexander was sent to Burma (in spring 1942) to take command of the territory threatened by the Japanese. Here he organized another successful retreat, (the longest in the history of the British Army) in spite of Japanese superiority.

Wladyslaw Anders

On 15 August 1942 Churchill appointed him Commander-in-Chief Middle East. Placed under him was General Montgomery, the new commander of the British 8th Army; Montgomery described Alexander as the only man under whom any General would gladly serve in a subordinate position. Victory at El Alamein was followed by final victory in the desert.

After the Allied forces of Operation 'Torch' and the Western Desert Forces had joined up in Tunisia in February 1943, Alexander became Deputy to General Eisenhower and Commander-in-Chief of the 18th Army Group, the Anglo-American land forces in Tunisia. As such Alexander also commanded the Allied land forces (15th Army Group) of Operation 'Husky', the descent on Sicily on 10 July 1943. When General Eisenhower was seconded to London as Allied Commander-in-Chief for the invasion of France, General Alexander was appointed Commander-in-Chief Allied Forces in Italy.

Wladyslaw Anders

The commander of the Polish II Corps, adored by his soldiers who took Monte Cassino, was born at Błonie near Warsaw on 11 August 1892. From 1911 to 1914 he studied at the Polytechnic in Riga. On the outbreak of the First World War he became Ensign of the Reserve in the Russian 3rd Dragoon Regiment. Decorated for bravery with the St. George's Cross, he attended the General Staff Academy in Petersburg until February 1917.

After the outbreak of the Russian Revolution and the re-grouping of the Polish units he first commanded the 1st Lancer Regiment, and then was promoted Chief-of-Staff of the 1st Rifle Division. Fighting against the Red Army, Anders was in command of the 15th Lancer Regiment during the Polish-Soviet War of 1919–21 and received the highest Polish decorations for bravery.

In September 1939 as commander of the *Nowogrodzka Brygada Kawalerii* (a cavalry brigade), he fought against Hitler's troops from Lidzbark on the East Prussian border to Sambor in southern Poland. When the Soviet Union invaded Poland (17 September 1939) he fought against the Red Army, which cut off his brigade's retreat to Hungary. Wounded three times and on crutches, he was taken prisoner by the Soviets on 29 September 1939 and brought to Moscow. There he spent twenty months in the notorious prisons of Lubyanka and Butyrki, seven of them in solitary confinement. After the agreement between Stalin and the Polish government in exile in London he was released – wearing only shirt and underpants. From 10 August 1941 he held the rank of divisional general.

As Commander of the Polish forces in the Soviet Union, Anders assembled a Polish army, in extremely difficult conditions, from those Polish citizens who had been deported to Russia. Intimately acquainted with the grim possibilities within the Soviet Union, he immediately set about evacuating his troops and their families to Iran. From September 1942 he commanded the Polish Army in the Middle East, and in this capacity was in charge of the Polish II Corps from July 1943. On 23 March 1944 he undertook the task of conquering Monte Cassino, which brought him and his soldiers the most significant Polish victory of the Second World War.

Mark Clark

Bernard Freyberg

Mark Clark

Commander-in-Chief of the US 5th Army and one of the most controversial generals of the Italian campaign; good-looking, outspoken and with star qualities, Mark Clark had a unique gift for generating personal publicity by means of a posse of accompanying war correspondents.

Mark W. Clark was born in Madison Barracks, New York on 1 May 1896, the son of a colonel in the US Army. He was educated at West Point, which he left in 1917, and as a captain (temporary) in the 11th Infantry Regiment he took part in the fighting in France from June 1918 in the Vosges sector.

He was promoted to major in August 1933, and attached to the General Staff School at Fort Leavenworth. Not until 1940 did he become lt.-colonel; in April 1942 he was made maj.-general, and one month later was Chief-of-Staff of the Army Ground Forces. From July 1942, based in England, Clark commanded all US troops in Europe. In November 1942 he landed on the Algerian coast after a hazardous journey in a dinghy put out by the British submarine *Seraph* in order to prepare for Operation 'Torch'.

Clark received his first army command in January 1943, that of the US 5th Army. With this force he landed in Sicily on 10 July 1943 (Operation 'Husky') and at Salerno on 9 September 1943 (Operation 'Avalanche').

Bernard Freyberg

Commander of the New Zealand II Corps, and the man at whose insistence the ancient abbey of Monte Cassino was destroyed, Freyberg was famous for his personal bravery.

Born in Richmond (Surrey) on 21 March 1889, he fought in France during the First World War and rose to the rank of brigadier. By his vigorous intervention at Bailleul during the German summer offensive of 1918 and by personally taking part in the action, Freyberg succeeded

Alphonse Juin

at the last moment in sealing off an extremely dangerous gap in the British front. That gained him Great Britain's highest wartime decoration, the Victoria Cross.

At the beginning of the Second World War, in November 1939, Freyberg commanded the New Zealand forces and took part with them in the fighting in Greece. After the German attack on Greece he withdrew his troops and was appointed by Churchill Commander-in-Chief Allied Forces in Crete. Here, too, Freyberg was able to save half of his 30,000 soldiers after the daring German airborne invasion. Then he was set against Rommel in North Africa.

Encircled by the Germans at Marsa Matrûh, Freyberg broke out with his troops in spite of being badly wounded. Immediately on his recovery he returned to his division and fought at El Alamein, and from April to August 1943 he commanded the British X Corps. Wounded thirty-six times in all, Freyberg had unrivalled experience by 1944, for he was the only senior field commander from the First World War to serve as such throughout the Second World War.

As he was responsible to the New Zealand government and not to Churchill, Freyberg had more freedom of action than other divisional commanders in Europe. The responsibility which he carried for his men was immense, however. His troops were a very high proportion of the entire male population of New Zealand of military age, and Freyberg cared for his soldiers like a father.

Alphonse Juin

Commander of the *Corps expéditionnaire français* (CEF), which he led with verve and success, Juin knew the rules of mountain warfare like no other Allied commander and was instrumental in restoring military prestige to the *'Grande Nation'*.

Born in Bône (Annaba) in Eastern Algeria on 16 December 1888, Juin went to the Military Academy at St. Cyr and, as the robust son of a gendarme, competed with the sons of the aristocracy for the distinction of being the best cadet, which he achieved, together with de Gaulle and de Lattre de Tassigny, in 1912. During the First World War he fought in Flanders and Champagne, where his right hand was shot to pieces in 1915. Then he became Liaison Officer with the US Army in France. In 1920–22 he taught at the *École de Guerre*, and this was followed by a post as Chief-of-Staff to the legendary conqueror of Morocco, Marshal Lyautey, with whom he helped to subdue the Rifs. In 1931 he became military advisor to the Resident General in Rabat, in 1935 commander of the 3rd Zouave Regiment, and in 1937 he joined the general staff and was promoted to general.

During the German attack in May 1940 Juin fought in Belgium and at Lille, where he was taken prisoner by the Germans. In 1941 he was released at Marshal Pétain's request, and a few months later became Commander-in-Chief of the Vichy Forces in North Africa instead of General Weygand. After the Allied landing in Morocco and Algeria Juin placed himself at the side of General de Gaulle and on 27 December 1942 became Commander-in-Chief of the French Forces in North Africa. Then he took over the *Corps expéditionnaire français* with which he landed at Naples at the end of November 1943.

His colonial troops – particularly the warriors from the Atlas Mountains – won the most important French victory of the Second World War in the Abruzzi in May 1944.

Henry Maitland Wilson

Henry Maitland Wilson

Good-humoured and known as Jumbo on account of his size, Wilson was Allied Commander-in-Chief Mediterranean Theatre during the fighting around Monte Cassino. Of all the Allied Commanders he had the most experience in the area.

Born in 1889, he came to Egypt in 1939 in the first phase of the war as General-Officer-Commanding, in order to work out the plan for an operation against Italian North Africa (Libya). Then he became commander of the British Expeditionary Corps in Greece. On 6 June 1941 the Commonwealth Forces under General Wilson attacked the French Vichy Forces in Syria, who capitulated on 3 July 1941. On 15 September 1942 Wilson assumed the Persia and Iraq Command (PAIC), and from 16 February 1943 he replaced General Alexander as Commander-in-Chief of the British Middle East Forces. On 24 December 1943 he received the appointment of Commander-in-Chief Mediterranean Theatre.

Wilson supported the plan to occupy the Aegean Islands after the collapse of Italy and was an advocate of the Anzio landings.

Albert Kesselring

Albert Kesselring

Generalfeldmarschall der Luftwaffe (Marshal of the Air Force), Kesselring was able to convince Hitler, against Rommel's advice, that Italy had to be defended south of Rome.

Born in Lower Franconia on 20 November 1885, Kesselring, who came from a brewer's family, joined the 3rd Bavarian Foot-Artillery Regiment (Metz) as an ensign in 1904. By 1907 he was a lieutenant. After training at the school of gunnery and engineering in Munich he became a specialist in surveying and flash-spotting. At the beginning of the First World War, he was First Lieutenant of his company, but rose through different staff posts, until finally he was on the general

Fridolin von Senger und Etterlin

staff. In 1919 joined the *Reichswehr* as acting commander of III Bavarian Corps (Nuremberg).

On 1 October 1922 Kesselring transferred to the *Heeresleitung* (Army High Command) in Berlin, and in 1930 was Colonel of the 4th Artillery Regiment (Dresden).

From 1 October 1933 he was *Verwaltungschef* (director) of the new *Luftfahrtkommissariat* (Air Commission). From June 1936 he was *Chef des Generalstabs der Luftwaffe* (Chief of the German Air Staff), and in charge of the entire *Fliegerausbildungswesen* (Air force personnel training). Kesselring also organized the AA and signals troops. On 1 June 1937 as a *General der Flieger* (Air General) he commanded *Luftkreis III* (Dresden). From October 1938 he became *Chef der Luftwaffengruppe* (*Luftflotte I*) in Berlin. In September 1939 *Luftflotte I* was assigned to *Heeresgruppe Nord* (Army Group North) and played a decisive part in the fighting against Poland.

In January 1940 Kesselring assumed command of *Luftflotte II* (Western Front), and on 19 July 1940 was directly promoted to *Generalfeldmarschall* (Air Chief Marshal). In the Battle of Britain during the summer of 1940, his *Luftflotte II* suffered a painful defeat, however. For the invasion of the Soviet Union (22 June 1941) *Luftflotte II* was sent into action with *Heeresgruppe Mitte* (Army Group Centre). From 5 December 1941 he was Commander-in-Chief of the German Air Force in the Mediterranean and North Africa. From 1943 he was Commander-in-Chief of the *Wehrmacht* in the southern theatre of war.

Fridolin von Senger und Etterlin

The artistic and sensitive commanding general of XIV Panzer Corps, whose men had the task of defending the Gustav Line in the Cassino sector, was born in Waldshut on 4 September 1891. Aged nineteen he joined the 5th/76th Baden Field Artillery Regiment on 10 October 1910 as a volunteer, then went to the University of Oxford as a Rhodes Scholar. In 1914 he was a lieutenant in the reserve, and was called for active service on 27 June 1917. At the end of the First World War he entered the *Reichswehr* as Adjutant or *Eskadronschef* (squadron commander) in the 18th Cavalry Regiment (Bad Cannstatt). On 1 January 1927 he was promoted to *Rittmeister* (captain of cavalry); on 1 August 1936, lt.-colonel; on 10 November 1938 commander of the 3rd Cavalry Regiment and on 1 March 1939 he became a colonel. From November 1939 he was commander of the 22nd Cavalry Regiment, and from 2 February 1940 he led the 2nd Cavalry Brigade.

In the campaign in the West von Senger led the '*Schnelle Brigade von Senger*', and from July 1940 until July 1942 was head of the German delegation to the Italian-French Armistice Commission (Turin). On 1 September 1941 he became a major-general, and on the Eastern Front from 10 October 1942 commanded the 17th Panzer Division; on 1 May 1943 he was promoted lt.-general. From June 1943 he directed German troops on Sicily, and from August 1943 was commander of German troops on Sardinia and Corsica. He directed the evacuation of these three islands with great success, and from 8 October 1943 von Senger and Etterlin took command of XIV Panzer Corps. On 1 January 1944 he was promoted to Panzer general.

The well known anti-Nazi feelings of this anglophile General – he was also a lay member of the Benedictine Order – led to the devaluation of his contribution to the defence of Cassino; it was scarcely mentioned by Nazi propaganda and represented as insignificant.

Heinrich von Vietinghoff-Scheel

Heinrich-Gottfried von Vietinghoff-Scheel

Commander-in-Chief of the German 10th Army, Vietinghoff was a very accomplished, skilful and adaptable mediator between the troops and High Command, although not particularly popular with the ordinary soldier.

He was born in Mainz on 6 December 1887, and by 1898 was a cadet. On 6 March 1906, when aged nineteen, he became an ensign in the Prussian Army and one year later, on 27 January 1907, became Lieutenant in the 2nd *Garde-Grenadierregiment*. After the outbreak of the First World War he was made *Truppenoffizier* (troop officer) and in 1915 captain in the general staff of the *Oberste Heeresleitung* (German Army Command). In 1919 he joined the *Reichswehr* and in 1921 he became company commander in the 9th Infantry Regiment. From 1 March 1926 he was a major on the staff of the 2nd Infantry Division (Stettin). In 1929 he transferred to the *Wehramt* (Defence Ministry); from 1 February 1931 he was Lt.-Colonel and Commanding Officer of the 1st Battalion in the 14th Infantry Regiment.

On 1 April 1933 came his promotion to colonel, and from February 1934 Vietinghoff became head of the *Abteilung Landesverteidigung* (Civil Defence Forces), by 1 April 1936 he was a maj.-general and two years later, on 1 march 1938, lt.-general. On 24 November 1938 he assumed command of the newly-formed 5th *Panzerdivision*, which he led in the Polish campaign of September 1939. From 21 October 1939 he was commanding general of XIII Army Corps, and on 1 June 1940 Panzer general. From 1 November 1940 until 10 June 1942 he commanded XXXXVI Panzer Corps and, deputizing for Colonel-General Model, the 9th Army. Then on 1 December 1942 he was made Commander-in-Chief of the 15th Army and on 15 August 1943 took over the 10th Army in Sicily.

PROLOGUE

Opposite: British soldiers dive for cover during the advance through Calabria. The Germans used delaying tactics wherever possible – but never risked major engagements.

Enemy Operations on the Coast of Calabria

Rome, Friday 3 September 1943
Italian Supreme Command reports: After the enemy's scattered attempts at invasion over the past few days had been beaten back, he began full-scale operations in the straits of Messina last night, against the coast of Calabria. Enemy convoys and ships lying at anchor in the harbours of Catania and Augusta were attacked by German aircraft to good effect. Formations of enemy aircraft dropped numerous bombs on Bolzano, Trento, Bologna and the area around Naples, which caused particular damage in Bologna . . .

Forward to Victory!

Friday 3 September 1943
General Montgomery to 8th Army
1. Having Captured SICILY as our first slice of the Italian home country, the time has now come to carry the battle on to the mainland of Italy.
2. To the Eighth Army has been given the great honour of being the first troops of the Allied Armies to land on the mainland of the continent of Europe.
3. I want to tell all of you, soldiers of the Eighth Army, that I have complete confidence in the successful outcome of the operations we are now going to carry out.

We have a good plan, and air support on a greater scale than we have ever had before.

There can only be one end to this battle, and that is: ANOTHER SUCCESS.

4. Forward to Victory!
   Let us knock ITALY out of the war!
5. Good luck. And God Bless you all.

Italy Invaded

Saturday 4 September 1943
The Times *reports:* British and Canadian troops of the Eighth Army have landed on the mainland of Italy in Calabria, and late last night a correspondent at Allied Headquarters in North Africa reported that reinforcements are being poured into the toe of Italy.

Apart from this message, no news from official sources had been issued up to an early hour this morning, but our Correspondent in Algiers stated that the invasion has met with no opposition from the air.

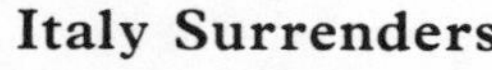

Italy Surrenders

Marshal Badoglio, who led Italy out of the war.

Wednesday 8 September 1943
General Eisenhower on Algiers Radio: This is General Dwight D. Eisenhower, Commander-in-Chief of the Allied forces in the Mediterranean.

The Italian Government has surrendered its forces unconditionally. As Allied Commander-in-Chief I have granted a military armistice, the terms of which have been approved by the Governments of the United Kingdom, the United States, and the Union of Soviet Socialist Republics. I am thus acting in the interests of the United Nations.

The Italian Government has bound itself to abide by these terms without reservation. The armistice was signed by my representative and the representative of Marshal Badoglio, and it becomes effective this instant. Hostilities between the armed forces of the United Nations and those of Italy terminate at once.

All Italians who now act to help eject the German aggressor from Italian soil will have the assistance and support of the United Nations.

Allied Surrender Terms

Wednesday 8 September 1943
General Maitland Wilson announces to the Italian people: Your Government has signed an armistice, and the war between Italy and the United Nations is over. Conforming with the armistice conditions, I give the following orders, which must immediately be complied with by all members of the Italian armed forces in the Balkans and Aegean:

First, all hostile acts towards the population of the countries in which you are must cease forthwith.

A German machine-gun mounting designed for anti-aircraft work. Allied air superiority in southern Italy gave the German High Command immense problems in the supply and transport of its forces.

Secondly, every unit must maintain its strictest discipline and keep its actual formations.

Thirdly, every attempt by Germans or their satellites to disarm or disband Italian forces, to take possession of their arms, stores, petrol, and water, or points in which they are situated, must be resisted by force of arms. All German orders will be disregarded.

Fourthly, Italian troops shall take possession by force of all points occupied by Germans in the Dodecanese.

Fifthly, all units of the mercantile marine and fleet will proceed immediately as follows:- The mercantile fleet at any point east of 17 degrees will proceed directly to Alexandria and may dock at a United Nations port for refuelling. Warships will proceed direct to Haifa.

Sixthly, all Italian aircraft will fly immediately to Nicosia, Derna, Tobruk, and El Adem.

Failure to comply with this order, or any orders which I shall give in future, will be considered as violation of the armistice terms accepted by your supreme commander and will prejudice your future treatment.

Disarmament of Italian Troops

Friday 10 September 1943
German Supreme Command announces: In recent weeks the treacherous Badoglio government has assembled strong forces in Rome in preparation for its defection, and placed the city itself on the defensive against the German troops positioned outside Rome. The danger of an enemy landing west of Rome was given as justification. After Italy's capitulation on 8 September, fighting broke out between German and Italian troops. The German Commander-in-Chief South, Field-Marshal Kesselring, brought up reinforcements, led the attack on Rome and presented the Italian commander with an ultimatum. Under this pressure the Italian Commander-in-Chief in Rome surrendered inside a radius of 50km (30 miles). Disarming of the Italian troops is now underway, and communications with the German army in the area around Naples and Salerno have been established.

British infantry of the 46th Division cautiously move around a burning German Mark IV tank on the road towards Salerno.

German Bitterness

Friday 10 September 1943
Radio Beromünster (Switzerland) reports: 8 September 1943 will go down in the history of the Second World War as a black day for Germany. For on 8 September the Russian army won back the Donets basin and its capital of Stalino, and the armistice between the Allied Powers and Italy came into force. While crowds in Moscow greeted the recovery of Russia's greatest industrial and mining region with rejoicing, the news of Italy's capitulation produced joyful demonstrations in the streets of London and New York. The German people received the news of their Axis partner's defection with corresponding bitterness, and the German public had no illusions about the gravity of this simultaneous advance on the southern and eastern fronts by enemy forces . . .

The precipitate events of the last forty-eight hours were produced by the announcement from Eisenhower's headquarters that he had secured a military armistice with Italy which had already been approved by the British, American and Soviet governments; that the Italian government had already declared itself willing to submit to these conditions; and that the armistice would come into force at once and hostilities would cease immediately.

Secret Report of the SS Security Service on the Internal Political Situation

Monday 13 September 1943 (green series)
Reports on the Führer's *speech and the events in Italy:* Reports from all parts of the *Reich* confirm the first impression which the *Führer's* speech and the German action in Italy had aroused. The people's self-confidence, which was temporarily shaken, has returned. Confidence in the *Führer* has reached new heights.

Statements by the *Führer* to the effect that what has occurred in Italy is impossible in Germany, since he can depend upon his marshals, admirals and generals, were received with pride, just as the speech has strengthened the national pride of the German people in general.

The German successes announced so far probably make it appear to the population that no more unpleasant military surprises are to be expected from Italy's treachery.

There is certainly anxiety, especially among women, about the fate of German troops in southern Italy. Besides that there is anxiety that the fighting in Italy requires troops who will be missed on the Eastern Front. The people's attitude to the expected treatment of the Vatican is problematic. Ideologically sound National Socialists were pleased to learn that German troops had taken over the defence of the Vatican, explaining that under the protection of the *Leibstandarte Adolf Hitler* the Vatican would cease to be a centre of espionage. As an officer summed it up: 'Now the Pope is nearer to Himmler than to heaven (*Himmel*).' [*'Nun ist der Papst dem Himmler näher als dem Himmel'*]

The *Wehrmacht* will take over the defence of Vatican City. In northern Italy, after a short but extremely bitter fight, Field-Marshal Rommel and the divisions of his army group forced the Italian units to surrender.

In conclusion the reports show that morale has been greatly raised by the successes in Italy and the speech by the *Führer*.

Cosenza Taken

Tuesday 14 September 1943
Allied Force Headquarters announces: On the Eighth Army front progress is rapid. The town of Cosenza has been taken. Our troops are continuing their advance unchecked except by demolitions.

Heavy fighting continues on the Fifth Army front. The Germans are counter-attacking desperately and, at certain points, have regained some of the ground previously taken by us. North and west of Taranto our forces are active.

Salerno Beach-Head

Wednesday 15 September 1943
The Times *reports:* On the Salerno beach-heads the fighting grows ever more bitter as both sides have thrown fresh forces into the *mélée*. Along the whole 25-mile front within the arc of the mountains of which the beach forms the chord, the battle is one of ceaseless alternation of attack and counter-attack at one point or another, with the line continually moving to and fro. At the time the *communiqué* issued this morning was written we were losers on the day's balance. To-day may have restored our gains, but the Germans, in spite of the North-West African Air Force's concentration of almost its whole strength against the two enemy routes of approach to the bridgehead from Naples and from Calabria, have been reinforced, and in the air are markedly stronger and more active, at least according to the ground troops' report.

A 'Second Front'

Friday 17 September 1943
Radio Beromünster reports: The speed with which the *Wehrmacht* stepped into the hiatus caused by Italy's withdrawal from the war

indicate that the six weeks which elapsed between the fall of facism and the conclusion of the armistice between Italy and the Allies were utilized by the German Supreme Command to prepare for Italy's expected defection and the altered front . . .

The week which has gone by since the armistice came into force has shown that the advancing Allied forces which landed in southern Italy must be prepared for resolute and fierce resistance from the Germans. A 'Second Front' in the truest sense has opened there, and for the first time on the continent of Europe, Anglo-Saxons and Germans are facing each other across an important land front where the conquest or defence of one of the greatest countries in Europe is at stake. Judging from the way things have developed since Italy's capitulation the fighting in Italy is likely to go on for a long time.

Corsica Liberated

Friday 24 September 1943
Radio Beromünster reports: Since German troops left the island of Sardinia during the week in face of the hostile actions of the Italian units stationed there, the valuable sea and air bases of this large Italian island in the western Mediterranean can be counted as a significant gain for the Allied strategy against central Italy. In Corsica too, the first independent operation by the Free French under General Giraud has taken place; and from Corsica short-range aircraft can reach the

US troops and equipment land in the Salerno beachhead. Such reinforcements were essential for Clark's hard-pressed forces.

beaches of Nice, Genoa, Spezia and Leghorn. Corsica is the first *département* of France where the civil servants of the Vichy government have been relieved by those of the French Committee of National Liberation.

8th Army Lands at Termoli

Tuesday 5 October 1943

The Times *reports:* The Eighth Army's landing at Termoli was made with tanks on Saturday night. Termoli is at the extreme north-east end of the lateral roads which cross Italy from north-east to south-west to join the Volturno River near Capua – a line which the Germans apparently intend to defend. Our land patrols are in touch with the landing party, but there is little news of the course of the fighting except that we have taken 60 prisoners and have established a firm footing.

The German units manning the line would seem to include a parachute division, the 29th Panzer Grenadier Division, the 26th Panzer Division, and, between Naples and the Volturno River, the

Soldiers of the British 8th Army bargain with an Italian peasant in Calabria. Despite having been at war with Britain for three years, the Italian people bore little animosity towards the Allies, who they saw as liberators.

Hermann Göring Division. The Hermann Göring and 26th Divisions took heavy punishment at Salerno.

The Eighth Army's progress, already hampered by demolition, has been made more difficult by rains.

Germans Evacuate Naples

Friday 8 October 1943
Radio Beromünster reports: Naples fell to the Allies a week ago, and during the last few days this has begun to effect the course of military operations on the southern front. Field-Marshal Kesselring is visibly restricting himself in order to gain time, and for that reason German resistance north of Naples, on the west and east coast of southern Italy and in the mountains is taking on the appearance of delaying tactics. The dreadful fate of Naples certainly shows the unrelenting thoroughness with which the retreating German troops are following their 'scorched earth policy'. This does, in fact, hinder the pursuing Allies considerably, as it even includes the destruction of the domestic water supply.

A British mortar crew in action admidst the ruins of an Italian village. The mortar crew was an integral part of the infantry combat team, although because of their smooth bore and low muzzle velocity, mortars themselves were not very accurate.

Disaster at Bari

Thursday 20 January 1944
The Times *reports:* Details were released yesterday of the sinking of 17 allied ships in the Adriatic port of Bari one night last October. The disaster was caused by two ammunition ships being hit by German bombs. The enemy, until the allied announcement, had no idea of the damage he had caused and claimed only that three ships had been sunk.

Slow Allied Progress

Friday 12 November 1943
Radio Beromünster reports: In Italy the co-ordinated moves by the American 5th Army and the British 8th Army have made only slow progress. The present front line is about as far from Rome as Geneva is from Berne. In between lie the southern spurs of the Apennines, the Alban Hills and the Abruzzi. What is noticeable about the Anglo-American presence on Italian soil is the fact that they are conducting this campaign with relatively modest forces, which explains the slowness of these operations even more satisfactorily than does the topography.

Foul Weather Along the Front

Thursday 18 November 1943
The Times *reports:* Snow on the Apennines and high winds and foul weather from the Adriatic coast to the Tyrrhenian Sea, slowed down all movement beyond local skirmishing along the allied front in Italy.

An enemy patrol which crossed the Garigliano river near its estuary on the left flank of the Fifth Army was caught making its way back, and severely shot up by our own forward elements. Immediately north of Venafro, United States troops, who had been compelled on the previous day to yield some ground on a hill, recovered most of it, and re-established their positions. South-west of Rionero, near the junction of the Fifth and Eighth Armies, a dozen or more German prisoners were captured in patrol fighting. There has been no change on the Eighth Army front beyond a slight improvement in our positions just north of Atessa.

German Counter-Attacks

Friday 3 December 1943
The Times *reports:* On the Fifth Army front the rain was less persistent, but there were frequent heavy showers. Four miles north of

Venafro the enemy launched a vigorous counter-attack near Filigrano the night before last which was repulsed by American troops. South-west of Mignano another counter-attack was beaten off by the Americans. It can now be mentioned that the United States 34th Division is operating in Italy. It is the division which landed at Algiers under General Ryder last year, saw much fighting in Tunisia, and was the first reinforcing division to land after the allied attack on Salerno.

Guarantee for the Abbey of Monte Cassino

Thursday 9 December 1943
Stefani's Agency reports: It is rumoured from the Vatican that the Pope has obtained an assurance from the warring powers that the hill on which the abbey of Monte Cassino stands will not be fortified, and nor will it be exposed to attacks from the air.

American Rangers of the 5th Army equipped with a 60mm M2 mortar which had a maximum range of nearly 2,000 yards and a rate of fire of 18 rounds per minute.

December 1943: A woman and child graphically display the strain of war. The people of the small towns and villages of central Italy were now caught up in the war with a vengeance.

San Pietro Taken

Monday 20 December 1943

The Times *reports:* On the Fifth Army front American troops have captured the village of San Pietro, which the Germans had fortified into a defensive stronghold, just north of the Capua-Rome road beyond Mignano. The village was taken on Saturday afternoon after three days and nights of bitter struggle, in which the American infantry showed great qualities of courage, determination, and endurance. It is about 800ft. up, on a steep hill, and supplies could be taken forward only by man-handling, even mules being unable to reach many of the hilltop positions.

The Germans fought desperately to retain this key point in their defence of the Rome road. Their casualties are stated to be very heavy and they abandoned quantities of small arms and ammunition. The United States casualties are described as moderate.

Wartime Christmas

Friday 24 December 1943

Radio Beromünster reports: Whoever has the extraordinary good fortune to be spending Christmas today in a peaceful family setting by a Christmas tree will not fail to think of the thousands and millions of fellow human beings to whom this war has brought unspeakable suffering and anguish. For no-one can be so unfeeling as not to be keenly aware of the irreconcilable contrast between the message of Christmas and the most remorseless of all wars.

Torrential Rain

Sunday 2 January 1944
Allied Force Headquarters announces: Torrential rain and high winds curtailed activity on most of the front of the 15th Army Group in Italy. Canadian troops of the Eighth Army beat off a counter-attack in the Adriatic coastal sector, and captured the village of San Tommaso. British troops of the Fifth Army staged a successful raid into enemy positions. American troops in the mountains consolidated positions previously gained.

Patrols in Action Against Enemy

Tuesday January 4 1944
Allied Force Headquarters announces: Indian troops of the Eighth Army improved their position by seizing a prominent feature overlooking the enemy lines. Strong Fifth Army patrols clashed with the enemy.

A victim of the torrential rains, a field gun of the 7th Canadian Division remains firmly stuck in the mud despite the efforts of its crew. The severe weather greatly hampered the Allied advance and gave ample time for the Germans to improve their defensive lines.

An American-built truck struggles through a sea of mud on an Italian road. In these conditions, logistic problems became a major brake on Allied operations.

Enemy to Make a Stand

Wednesday 5 January 1944
The Times *reports:* On the Fifth Army front American patrols have probed German defences around the village of San Vittore, just north of the Rome road east of Cassino; here it is confirmed that the enemy is prepared to make as strong a stand as at San Pietro, similarly situated along the line of advance and now in our hands. East of Acquafondata some six miles north of San Vittore, Fifth Army patrols have also found enemy positions very firmly held along the mountain ranges.

Street Fighting in San Vittore

Thursday 6 January 1944
Allied Force Headquarters announces: On Wednesday American and British troops of the Fifth Army launched an attack in rough mountain country. Advances averaging a mile in depth were made along a front of approximately 10 miles. Street fighting is in progress in San Vittore, where the enemy has converted the houses into pill-boxes. In the Adriatic coastal sector stiff fighting continues.

Bitter Enemy Resistance

Saturday 8 January 1944
The Times *reports:* The Fifth Army attack east of Cassino on each side of the road to Rome continues. It is a slow, arduous assault against bitter enemy resistance, and is impeded further by heavy snowfalls in the mountains and lesser heights across which lies the way of British and American troops in this sector.

Short advances have been achieved in most parts of the ten mile line along which the attack has been launched. In San Vittore village which was captured by American troops in the initial assault, the Germans are now concentrating their powerful and determined defence within three strong-points. All approaches to the village and to the area around it, except for the enemy's single passage of withdrawal, are being heavily shelled by German artillery. South of the road British troops are advancing towards the River Garigliano, where, in this region, another 79 prisoners have been taken.

San Vittore Taken

Monday 10 January 1944
The Times *reports:* The Fifth Army in its attack along the road to Rome has fought its way through about one-third of the enemy's defensive positions which cover Cassino. San Vittore has been captured and American troops have pushed on to the next village.

British troops of the 5th Army carry boats forward. Such craft were essential to Allied offensives, for the series of rivers crossing the line of advance northward were often unfordable, and the Germans had destroyed all bridges.

Advance Towards Cassino

Wednesday 12 January 1944
The Times *reports:* Fifth Army forces in the south-western sector of the allied front in Italy have made a further advance towards Cassino along the road to Rome in occupying Monte di Piperni, about a mile north-east of Cervaro. They attacked from the east in the morning and met with stiff resistance from enemy forces, who later withdrew, and who had abandoned the height when the Americans made the final assault.

Battle for the Via Casilina

Saturday 15 January 1944
The Times *reports:* The long battle for the Via Casilina, the road to Rome, pursues its arduous course. American troops of the Fifth Army repulsed a fierce enemy counter-attack launched during the night and aimed at recapturing Cervaro, just north of the road. They have now

pushed on towards the northern heights of Monte Trocchio on the other side of the Via Casilina. In the mountains between Venafro and Alfedena French and American forces have driven the enemy from positions along several ranges, and have advanced to a depth of two miles in some places. . . . In the northern part of the Fifth Army front French troops, continuing their attack in the mountains, have captured three more peaks. North of the mountain road between Colli and Atina the French captured the eastern slopes of the San Pietro mountain range. These newly gained positions are just above the Cardito, west of the Mainarde range, and to the south of the Abruzzi national park. The Germans launched two heavy counter-attacks in a desperate but unsuccessful effort to regain these heights, which dominate a big stretch of the Colli-Atina mountain road that here begins to run parallel, more or less, with the Via Casilina in the south.

British troops storm a house in southern Italy. Much of the fighting in the Italian campaign involved bitter house-to-house struggles which resulted in a high casualty rate for only limited territorial gains.

ON WEDNESDAY 5 MAY 1943, only a few months after the surrender of the 6th Army in Stalingrad, the British 1st Army began its decisive offensive on the Tunisian western front against the German 5th Panzer Army. The German front was breached and the remnants of the army split into two parts. Forty-eight hours later British troops occupied Bizerta and Tunis.

On Sunday 9 May 1943 the German Army High Command reported, 'Documents and equipment destroyed. . .' On 12 and 13 May 1943, cut off from all supplies, the rest of Army Group Africa (Colonel-General von Arnim) and the Italian 1st Army (Colonel-General Messe) likewise laid down their arms. 130,000 German and 120,000 Italian soldiers were taken prisoner. The fighting in North Africa was now at an end and the southern coast of the Mediterranean in Allied hands. This German defeat, together with the catastrophe of Stalingrad and the collapse of the battle of the Atlantic, marked the turning-point of the war.

Two months later, the Allies took their next major step, Operation 'Husky', the invasion of Sicily. On Saturday 10 July 1943 Allied units under the command of General Eisenhower landed on the south-east coast of the island. In places the troops of the Axis powers offered fierce resistance, especially the German 'Hermann Göring' Panzer Division. Yet after two days Syracuse and Augusta were captured by the Allies.

When the Fascist 'Grand Council' assembled on 25 July 1943 Mussolini was held responsible for these defeats. King Victor Emmanuel III appointed Marshal Badoglio as the new head of government; the Fascist Party was dissolved and the Fascist régime in Italy collapsed. The run of defeats, culminating in the conquest of Sicily, and the intensified Allied air offensive had destroyed the Italian people's will to resist. Marshal Badoglio admittedly gave an assurance that he wished to continue the war at Germany's side, but at the same time he began to negotiate secretly with the Allies, in order to end the war for Italy 'as soon as possible and by every expedient'. On Thursday 29 July 1943 German intelligence intercepted a wireless conversation between Churchill and Roosevelt in which a proclamation by General Eisenhower and the impending armistice with Italy were discussed. Two days later, on 31 July, Hitler issued his first directive concerning Italy's possible withdrawal from the war. Then, on Thursday 3 August 1943, the first personal contact took place in Lisbon between representatives of the Italian government and the Allies. And on 12 August 1943 Italian and Allied senior army officers met in the strictest secrecy in the Portuguese capital to discuss a separate armistice with Italy.

While *General der Panzertruppen* (Panzer General) Hube was

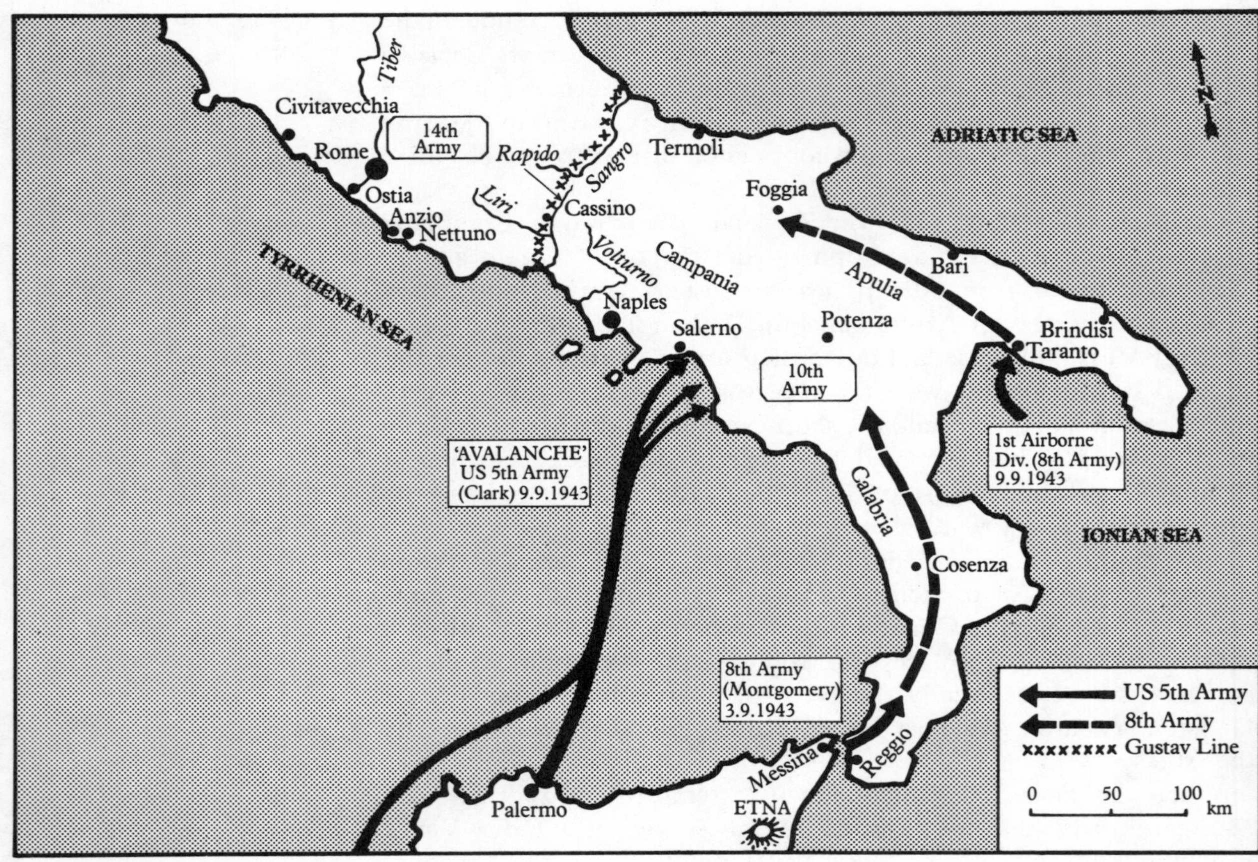

The Allied invasion of Italy

retreating from Sicily to the Italian mainland with his units, Badoglio conveyed to Allied headquarters at Algiers suggestions for a combined Allied-Italian operation against the German forces around Rome. Meanwhile Eisenhower was directed by Churchill and Roosevelt to accept Italy's unconditional surrender and gain the greatest possible advantage from it. It was hoped that he would establish air-bases around Rome and if possible in the north also; but the lack of ships and suitable troops made this order impracticable.

When the armistice negotiations started, in Cassible near Palermo (Sicily) on Tuesday 31 August 1943, new difficulties arose; the Italians would only sign if an Allied invasion north of Rome were to follow. To prepare for this operation General Taylor and Colonel Gardiner proceeded to Ustica, a small island north of Sicily. From here an Italian corvette picked them up and in this hazardous way both reached Rome. The planned landing of the US 82nd Airborne Division was not immediately possible however. Because fresh German troops were constantly arriving, the Italians explained, no airfield could

A section of the Royal Berkshire Regiment advances up a steep Italian hillside. The soldier on the right is armed with a Thompson submachine-gun; behind him is the section machine-gunner equipped with a Bren gun.

be kept open. In this situation Eisenhower could not agree to an air invasion, and for Badoglio there was no choice other than immediate acceptance of all the conditions. Failing such acceptance, American air attacks on all cities including Rome would follow. On Friday 3 September 1943 General Castellano signed the Cassible armistice though it was kept secret for the time being. It seemed to him most important for his country's future that the armistice should remain secret for as long as possible.

The conduct of the Allied campaign in Italy was entrusted to General Sir Harold Alexander, Commander-in-Chief of the 15th Army Group. This consisted of the British 8th Army (General B. L. Montgomery) and the recently formed US 5th Army (Lt.-General M. W. Clark). On the same day as the secret armistice was signed, 3 September, two divisions of the British 8th Army crossed the 5km ($3\frac{1}{2}$ miles) wide straits of Messina covered by an artillery barrage and landed near Reggio in south Calabria, a coastline where there were no mines or barbed wire entanglements. The British troops met little resistance and by the same evening had penetrated some kilometres into the interior. 3,000 Italian and three German stragglers were taken prisoner. The Italians willingly helped to unload the British landing craft.

In the next few days too, as the British pushed northwards, they met only delaying tactics which resulted in short engagements with German rearguards. However, numerous blown-up roads and demolished bridges held up the progress of the 8th Army. After four days, by 6 September, they had advanced only 45km (28 miles).

On Monday 8 September 1943 at 18.30 hours, as previously arranged, Eisenhower officially announced the Italian capitulation. Immediately, German Supreme Command (OKW) put into effect prepared counter-measures (Operation '*Achse*'): the occupation of Rome, and the disarmament, imprisonment or discharge of Italian troops in Italy, the south of France, Yugoslavia, Albania and Greece. At this time the Germans had sixteen divisions in Italy, divided into two army groups of eight divisions each. Army Group B (Field-Marshal Rommel) was stationed in northern Italy and Army Group C (Field-Marshal Kesselring) was south of Rome.

On Thursday 9 September at 04.25 hours, four divisions of the US 5th Army (Lt.-General Clark) landed on a flat sandy beach, 30km (19 miles) wide, in the bay of Salerno (Operation 'Avalanche'). This bay was the obvious place on southern Italy's craggy coast to launch an invasion, and the Allies were expected here by the Germans. They encountered fierce resistance from the 16th Armoured Division (Maj-General Sieckenius), part of the German 10th Army (Colonel-General von Vietinghoff), which had constructed fortress-like positions on the surrounding mountains. This area, 50km (31 miles) south of Naples, was just within range of the Allied fighters stationed on Sicily. The first Allied objective was Naples, the harbour which was to supply the advance towards Rome. The hope was to capture the Italian capital by Christmas 1943. But a day later German reinforcements rolled in: the 'Hermann Göring' Panzer Division (Lt.-General Conrath) and the 15th Panzer Grenadier Division (Maj-General Rodt).

On Sunday 12 September the Germans succeeded in freeing Mussolini, who was being held prisoner by Badoglio's troops. At 6am soldiers of the 1st Company (1st Lieutenant Baron von Berlepsch) of the Parachute Training Battalion and the *SS 'Friedenthal'* Commando (under SS-Major Otto Skorzeny) landed in transport gliders in front of the 'Campo Imperatore' Hotel in the Gran Sasso massif (Abruzzi), about 100km (62 miles) north of Rome. The guards offered no resistance. After a daring take-off, a Fieseler Storch piloted by Major Gerlach brought the Duce to Rome. Mussolini flew on via Vienna to Hitler's headquarters in East Prussia.

German paratroops advance through the streets of Naples during September 1943 supported by a Marder *self-propelled gun mounted on a Mark II tank chassis. Despite their status as élite troops the paratroops, in general, suffered from a shortage of artillery support weapons like the* Marder *shown here.*

On 13 September, when the German 26th Armoured Division (Lt.-General Baron von Lüttwitz) had arrived at Salerno, the Germans mounted a fierce counter-attack against the central sector of the Allied bridgehead, which was beaten off with the support of medium naval artillery and massed air attacks by nearly 6000 aeroplanes. On the same day, however, the US VI Corps (Maj.-General Dawley) was driven back to the beach on the Gulf of Salerno and German pressure was such that Lt.-General Clark prepared to re-embark with his headquarters staff. The turning-point came when Admiral Cunningham boldly decided to take the battleships *Warspite* and *Valiant* close into shore so that they could open fire on the German positions with their 15 inch guns.

By Thursday 16 September, Clark had received considerable reinforcements, and the German 10th Army now had to retreat behind the Volturno suffering from lack of fuel. In the fighting at Salerno the Allies had lost 15,000 of their best men; estimated losses had been far less. German losses totalled fewer than 8000 men.

There was no immediate danger to the German 14th Army (Colonel-

A dead German soldier, killed during fighting against the British 8th Army. The majority of battle casualties were caused by artillery fire, and British artillery was extremely efficient because of its advanced fire-control system.

General von Mackensen) from the British 8th Army, who were held up by German rearguards and a deep mined zone. The first divisions only reached Lagonegro on 15 September 1943, while the other units were still at Castrovillari.

At the same time Mussolini was forming a 'Republican Fascist Government' in northern Italy with its seat at Salò on Lake Garda.

The 8th Army did not join up with the 5th Army until Friday 17 September 1943. Three days later, on 20 September, the 8th Army occupied the important supply port of Bari. King Victor Emmanuel III, and the Badoglio government who had managed to escape from Rome, now moved into the town. A week later, on 27 September, the 8th Army captured Foggia. The thirteen airfields near the town formed the main base for the Allied strategic air forces, which could now attack the area under German control from the south. The airfields around Foggia had been one of the most important objectives of the Allied offensive in southern Italy. Amongst other things they put Allied bombers and fighter escorts within range of the oil-fields of Ploeşti in Romania, which were of vital importance to Germany.

Field-Marshal Kesselring now decided to return to intermediate positions, in order to prevent the Allies from taking the Italian capital for as long as possible. At the end of September Kesselring ordered the construction of the Reinhard Line, a defensive position which ran obliquely across Italy about 125km (75 miles) south of Rome, between the Garigliano and Sangro rivers and the town of Ortona on the Adriatic, and formed one of the strongest natural obstacles. The construction was carried out by Todt Organization workers led by a task force from German pioneer battalions. Most effort was put into the section on the coast of the Tyrrenhian sea, especially in the southern part where the Via Appia and the Via Casilina led to Rome.

A narrow defile near Mignano, guarded by the heights overlooking it, was of the utmost significance to the Germans. But should this forward line of defence have to be relinquished, the enemy could be stopped by another strong system of defence, the Gustav Line, which stretched from the lower Garigliano across the Rapido, (including the heights on both sides of Cassino and the Apennine ridge) up to the upper Sangro, and ended on the Adriatic near San Vito. The defences in depth also included the Liri valley, as well as another line which ran directly south between both coasts. The German 10th Army, which was to defend all these positions, was reinforced, and three divisions were ordered into the strong-point sectors of the Reinhard Line (known to the Allies as the Winter Line) and deployed for their construction.

On 1 October 1943, twenty-eight days after the landing at Salerno, the King's Dragoon Guards at last entered Naples. This occasioned Churchill to telegraph General Alexander that he hoped to meet him in

Indian soldiers of the 8th Army bring a 6 pdr anti-tank gun into position. The 4th Indian Division was one of the best formations of the 8th Army in Italy.

Rome at the end of the month, and simultaneously President Roosevelt telegraphed Marshal Stalin that Allied troops would shortly enter the Eternal City. On Monday 4 October 1943 the British 8th Army captured Termoli on the Adriatic coast, but by this time the 8th Army was being hit by a fuel shortage. Montgomery: 'On 4 October we had only 21 tons of petrol left in our depots, and the army was in danger of becoming immobilised'.

On the same day Hitler issued his directive to defend Italy along the Gaeta-Ortona line.

On Friday 8 October 1943 the US 5th Army reached the Volturno-Termoli line, and on Tuesday 12 October, after a four day lull in the

Monks from the abbey of Monte Cassino pack away the invaluable books of their library in preparation for their removal to safer surroundings in the Vatican.

fighting, advanced to attack the defence lines. The Volturno, swollen by the autumn rain and its bridges blown up by the Germans, now proved a major obstacle.

On Wednesday 13 October 1943 the Badoglio government declared war on Germany and was accepted by the Allies as a co-belligerent.

On Thursday 14 October Lt.-Colonel Schlegel, an Austrian commanding the engineer detachment of the 'Hermann Göring' Panzer Division, drove to Cassino. Unknown to his divisional commander, Lt.-General Conrath, Schlegel wished to warn the Abbot, Dom Gregorio Diamare, of the impending danger, and to persuade him to accept help in bringing the monastery's art treasures to safety. Schlegel explained to the Abbot that Monte Cassino would shortly be involved in the fighting. The Germans therefore wished to take all the portable works of art, the archives, manuscripts and the valuable library to a safe place. He indicated to the Abbot that the German main fighting line would go right over the monastery hill; yet the Abbot's sense of security could hardly be shaken. 'Airmen', he considered, 'would never destroy Monte Cassino'. Schlegel: 'I did not want to insist; I would abide by whatever the abbey might decide. I would return in two days to find out. With these words I rose and took my leave.'

On Friday 15 October 1943 the US 5th Army succeeded in forcing its way across the Volturno, but made painfully slow progress in the trackless mountains. German delaying tactics were always the same. They would defend a position for a time until the attacks became fiercer, then they would blow up the bridges, lay mine-fields and road blocks and retire to the next mountain village suitable for defence, always gaining time for the construction of the Gustav Line. Meanwhile heavy rain hampered the Allied advance.

On Saturday 16 October Lt.-Colonel Schlegel again drove to the Benedictine monastery. Schlegel:

> 'When I returned to Monte Cassino the situation had altered drastically. The war had come a great deal closer to the monastery. The Abbot now proved himself the gracious, upright man that he was. He begged me to help the monastery and said that he would do all he could to support my rescue work. I suggested that a lorry which I would send over the same day might first be loaded up with whatever he chose, and be driven to Rome escorted by two monks. When they had arrived and the lorry had been unloaded these two would hand an acknowledgement to the driver which I would then convey to the Abbot. My suggestion was gladly accepted and at once carried out.
>
> 'Next day, when I delivered the acknowledgement of the lorry's safe arrival in Rome, the Abbot capitulated completely. He urgently begged me to help in whatever way and as quickly as I could, and declared that all my orders would be carried out at once . . . First of all I sent over some lorries which were loaded up fairly indiscriminately by the monks and dispatched to Rome with the now customary escort of two monks to each. The Abbot was overjoyed to receive notice that they had duly arrived. It was high time to attack the evacuation of the library . . . What I needed were willing hands, materials and tools. In a nearby drink factory I found a number of chests and a large quantity of sawn-up wood. I had everything brought to Monte Cassino in lorries and procured nails to make more chests. From among the willing refugees who inhabited the monastery courtyard I now picked out suitable workers. I obtained full board for them from the monastery and gave them twenty cigarettes a day out of our army rations. My soldiers, who were carpenters and cabinet makers to a man, organized, supervised and generally increased production . . .'

Packing cases are constructed for the removal of the abbey's art treasures. The German propaganda service made great play of this exercise which presented the Germans as guardians of European Civilisation.

On Tuesday 19 October, the Allied offensive north of the Volturno came to a standstill in front of the German positions, but on Friday 22 October the British 8th Army, continuing its advance northwards along the Adriatic coast, forced its way across the Trigno.

Meanwhile, at the monastery, the rescue work continued. Schlegel again:

'In a few days, functioning almost like an assembly line, our carpenter's shop had made hundreds of chests as well as crates for pictures and packing-cases for particularly valuable items. As soon as it was finished each chest was taken to the library where it was filled with books, then loaded immediately on to a lorry . . . Even so, the monastery carpenter's shop turned out to be inadequate. I had to take the decision to transport whole lorry-loads of the big, handwritten monastery records protected only by carpets. But in this way we succeeded in saving 70,000 volumes from the library and archives.

'If I was primarily concerned to save the library, I was also making full use of the time available to safeguard the other valuables. Every lorry which I wrested from the front had to be filled to overflowing. Very many valuable pictures could not be crated, but travelled the road to Rome stacked up against each other, protected only by sheets . . .

'I had still not made any report to my general. It was clear that I should have done so, but it was less clear whether he would allow me to continue my rescue work.

'One morning a colonel appeared at the entrance to the monastery. I quickly went up to him and announced my name and unit and that I was engaged in evacuating the monks and art treasures of Monte Cassino. He asked whether I had been ordered to do this. "Yes", I answered untruthfully. "I have not come here to make an inspection", said the colonel, "but wanted to have a look at the monastery." He said goodbye quickly and disappeared. I was still deep in thought when a lorry ground to a halt in the sand at the gate. Twenty military policemen stormed into the monastery led by an officer.

'I went up to them. "What's the matter?"

"Monte Cassino is being plundered."

"Who says that?"

"Orders from High Command South."

"Report that I am the plunderer, but first speak to the monks."

'The error was cleared up in a moment, the officer apologized to the inmates of the monastery and to me and departed with his men. I did not know that the Allied radio stations were alarming the whole world with a report that the "Hermann Göring" Division was plundering the monastery.

'I was now faced with the unavoidable necessity of making an immediate report to my commanding general. In the end, he was in full agreement and ordered the work to be stepped up with the inclusion of a few members of the propaganda company to make permanent records of what was going on . . . The work was now going smoothly: carpenter's shop, loading and transport detachments were all functioning perfectly. The lorries were unloaded in Rome, either at San Paolo or San Anselmo. The monks who accompanied them remained in Rome and were thus brough to safety at the same time . . .'

The Nazi propaganda machine now made full use of this rescue operation.

On Monday 25 October 1943 the US 5th Army reached the Raviscanina-Francolise line, and paused north of the Agnena canals to prepare for an assault on the Reinhard Line. Torrential rain, icy mountain storms, almost impassable mud, and the lack of billets (destroyed by the retreating Germans) all combined to lower the morale of the Allied units, which in any case had been in action continuously since landing in Italy. Montgomery: 'The basic trouble was that we became involved in a major campaign lacking a predetermined master plan. We had not made in advance the administrative plans and arrangements necessary to sustain the impetus of our operations.'

The Cassino sector was under the control of Lt.-General von Senger und Etterlin. While the Allies were struggling northwards, his

A British soldier crouches in the ruins of a house in Raviscanina.

XIV Panzer Corps had the opportunity to add its own obstacles to the already formidable natural barriers, and the Germans set about their work with a grim efficiency.

The Via Casilina – the road to Rome – ran along the Liri valley, and the only way into the Liri valley was across the Rapido. The two rivers met at right angles; and in the angle between them stood the mountains. Monte Cassino itself overlooked both valleys, and so any advance through to Rome along the Liri valley was hardly practicable while hostile forces occupied the mountain.

There were three main areas in which the Germans set up defences. First of all, there was the Rapido valley. Extensive minefields and individual booby traps provided a deadly carpet through which the Allied troops would have to advance; and this was supplemented by dams and new water courses north of the town designed so that the Rapido – regularly swollen during the spring – could be used to flood the valley. Those Germans defending the valley itself were given shelters well sited in the ditches and hillocks of the farmland, and, where the Liri valley began, all the paraphernalia of military ingenuity was brought into play – farm buildings became strongpoints, tank turrets were dug in and every fortification was heavily protected.

Secondly, the mountains themselves were given a covering far more deadly but much less visible than the winter snow: well situated, mutually supporting machine-gun nests, mortar emplacements, infantry positions and artillery observation posts. All likely approach routes were prepared with mines, booby traps and warning signals.

Finally, the town itself became a military stronghold. A network of trenches and tunnels connected concealed pill-boxes and houses were reinforced with steel and concrete. Anti-tank guns, tanks, machine-guns and infantrymen were given all the protection they would need to sustain a long, bitter struggle. Yet the Germans of XIV Panzer Corps did not fortify the monastery itself. General von Senger und Etterlin:

> 'I had agreed not to fortify the monastery. No-one would like to be held responsible for the destruction of such a cultural monument for the sake of a tactical advantage . . . According to German views on tactics a conspicuous point like that is quite unsuitable for an observation post because it would only be safe from artillery fire up to the beginning of the main battle, at the latest . . .'

In fact this 516m (1700 feet) high corner pillar of the Liri valley had no vital military significance, as towards both the west and north a number of similar mountains dominated the plain and the broad valley of the Liri. Apart from that, Monte Cassino with its monastery on the summit, clung to the side of Monte Cairo, which, at 1600m (5250 feet),

German mines, rendered harmless, lie awaiting collection. Mine detection was a major, and urgent, task as soon as the front line had moved forward.

was three times as high and by nature offered very much better possibilities for observation.

On Friday 5 November 1943 the 5th Army, which had been increased to five American and three British divisions, reached the Garigliano and positioned itself outside Mignano, from which the heights of the pass could be reached.

The next day the Americans tried to capture the Mignano gap, the forward position on the Reinhard Line. This was a stretch of ground almost 10km (6 miles) long over which the Via Casilina forced its way through the mountains before coming to the open valley of the Rapido. Some commanding heights north of the Mignano gap were certainly gained in the tough fighting, but south of the defile the attack was at first beaten back. The powerful attacking forces of the 5th Army, pushing forward along the Via Casilina towards Mignano, gradually compelled the German XIV Panzer Corps to give way, despite a stubborn rearguard action. Now, however, the worst fears of the Allied High Command began to be realized. By taking advantage of the difficult, mountainous terrain the Germans were able to set up a dogged defence on the Garigliano, the strategically important river line between central and southern Italy.

On Monday 15 November 1943, after all attempts to dislodge the German XIV Panzer Corps from the main Reinhard Line had resulted in only a few localized successes, General Alexander decided to call his troops to a halt. This lull in the fighting again allowed the Germans to strengthen the Gustav Line. By Saturday 20 November 1943 the divisions of the 5th Army which had been fighting continuously since Salerno had had a short rest, and Lt.-General Clark made a fresh thrust in the direction of the Rapido. But progress was extremely slow. The simultaneous attack by the British 8th Army had to be postponed as, after ceaseless rain, the Sangro had overflowed.

On Sunday 21 November Field-Marshal Kesselring was appointed commander of Army Group C and took over the defence of Italy. Field-Marshal Rommel, who up to now had been commander in northern Italy was despatched to France with the staff of Army Group B to prepare for the expected Allied invasion. Army Group B was taken over by the 14th Army (Colonel-General von Mackensen). Kesselring was now not only responsible for the operational and tactical command but also held the title of *Höchster Territorial-Befehlshaber* (Supreme Commander Occupied Territories). The only posts not subordinate to his were that of *Höchster SS- und Polizei-Führer Italien* (Police and SS chief for Italy) and the SD positions, which were under the command of Himmler.

At last, on Saturday 27 November, the 8th Army began the attack which had been postponed for a week. After heavy artillery fire and

Military Police of the 8th Army put the finishing touches to a Bailey Bridge spanning the river Sangro, one of the major natural obstacles to British progress in Italy.

massed air attacks on the German positions the offensive on the lower Sangro swung into action. In three days of bitter fighting the Germans were driven back and the front was breached in several places; British units succeeded in establishing a few bridgeheads over the Sangro and in penetrating the Gustav Line as far as Ortona. On the Adriatic coast the German 65th Infantry Division was almost completely wiped out by the 1st Tactical Air Force (Air Marshal Coningham). But German units hurriedly transferred to the front were in time to prevent an operational breakthrough by the 8th Army and succeeded in bringing the British divisions to a halt. Pescara, the main objective of the operation, was not reached. This was General Montgomery's last offensive in Italy.

As the 8th Army made its attack across the Sangro in early December the US 5th Army tried again to force the Mignano gap by taking Monte Camino. Not before 200,000 shells had been expended on the mountain, which thoroughly earned its nickname of 'Million Dollar Hill', was the Mignano gap secured. And still Monte Trocchio, the 'last hill' before Cassino, remained to be stormed. To advance this far and to capture the 10km (6 mile) long Mignano gap, eight divisions had taken six weeks and lost 15,864 men.

In the late afternoon of 2 December 1943 ninety-six Ju 88 bombers from I and II *Gruppen of Kampfgeschwader** (Bomber Wing) 54 and I and II *Gruppen of Kampfgeschwader* 76 (about 100 bombers in all) took off from Villaorba and Aviano airports near Milan to attack Bari, an

* In the *Luftwaffe* a *Geschwader* was, in theory, composed of 120 aircraft of a single type. Apart from staff planes, it consisted of three *Gruppen*, which in turn each consisted of three *Staffeln* of ten to twelve aircraft. The *Staffel* was the equivalent of a British squadron; the *Gruppe* had no precise equivalent.

British officers look across the harbour at Bari, surveying the results of the successful raid by the German Luftwaffe.

important port of 250,000 inhabitants on the Adriatic coast east of Naples. Lieutenant M. Ziegler:

'In the late afternoon we flew off with two other planes as pathfinders. Our Ju 88s were laden with *Düppel* strips (for jamming radar) and flares to mark the targets. It was already dark when we crossed the coast south of Ravenna. We were to approach our target from the Adriatic. Level with Cape Rossa we went down to 7000m (23,000 feet) and found to our astonishment that the harbour at Bari was lit up as though it were peacetime. We began to drop the jamming strips and because the harbour was so brightly lit we could have saved ourselves the trouble of dropping flares.'

On that evening, more than thirty Allied ships lay in the harbour at Bari, and their cargoes, military equipment and supplies, were just being discharged. In order to speed up the work at the docks all the lights had heedlessly been switched on when darkness fell, and so the harbour was a clear target.

After the pathfinders had dropped their strips, thus putting the

Allied radar equipment out of action, German formations appeared over Bari almost unnoticed. The anti-aircraft guns did not open fire until 7.30 pm, when the aircraft were on their bombing runs and the bombs were already exploding in the harbour.

Not one searchlight attempted to intercept them, not one barrage balloon was protecting what was, at that moment, the most important supply port on the European continent, and not one single Allied fighter appeared over Bari. No German bombing operation had ever been carried out so easily: without casualties or problems of any kind. After direct hits two ammunition ships exploded so violently that window-panes were shattered up to a distance of 12km (8 miles) away. An oil pipeline on the quay was hit; the oil pouring out was ignited by the petrol from a burning tanker and spread out to form an enormous carpet of flame. Even the ships previously spared now went up in flames.

This attack, which only lasted twenty minutes, was one of the most successful of the war. Never, with the exception of Pearl Harbor, were so many ships sunk at one blow. Altogether, nineteen transports totalling 73,343 gross register tons were destroyed and seven seriously damaged. Army and navy losses came to over 1000 men. Weeks went by before the harbour became fully operational again.

That was the official part of the disaster; the second part of the tragedy was kept secret for decades after the war. When the attack began, the freighter *John Harvey* was against the pier, and seventeen other ships were tied up beside her or were lying at anchor. Apart from high explosives, her cargo consisted of about one hundred tonnes of heavy mustard gas in 100 pound (45.5kg) bombs; an extremely dangerous poison gas, illegal in international law. The Allied command wanted to have this weapon in their Italian arsenal 'just in case'.

At the very begining of the attack the *John Harvey* received a direct hit and went down with her entire crew. Although the gas bombs were not fused, many of them burst. The dangerous poison spread into the dock. The poison floating on the surface of the water became a lethal threat to the survivors of the attack, although fortunately most of it was driven out to sea. Many soldiers and sailors were pulled out of the contaminated water; but neither the rescue teams nor the rescued men suspected the presence of mustard gas. Military headquarters at the harbour knew of the dangerous cargo on board the *John Harvey* but in the chaos no-one thought of it. Some of the survivors remembered later that they had been aware of a 'smell of garlic' but no-one attached any significance to it. And in the overcrowded hospitals no-one was concerned about people who were smeared with oil but unhurt. Still in their sodden gas-soaked clothing, they were simply put wherever there was space. Two hours later the first of them were already complaining of frightful pains, which felt as though they had sand in their eyes.

The harbour authorities did not discover any of the mustard gas bombs until about twelve hours after the attack, and only then was the cargo of the *John Harvey* brought to mind. The hospitals were at once informed that a number of the rescued might possibly have come into contact with mustard gas. Eighteen hours after the attack the first fatality from the effect of the dangerous poison was reported. There were 617 contaminated men altogether, of whom eighty-three died, the last one not until a month after the attack.

If the rescue teams and doctors concerned had known that poison gases were involved, and if the appropriate measures had been taken at once, there would not have been so many deaths.

The case of the *Bistera* was also kept strictly secret. The *Bistera*, which was not damaged in the attack, fished thirty survivors out of the dock and, according to the instructions given by the harbour authorities, steamed to Taranto. Four hours later, on the open sea, the whole crew were overcome by unbearable eye pains. When the *Bistera* eventually reached Taranto eighteen hours after the attack, the almost completely blinded crew was scarcely able to tie up the ship. Churchill's order that the cause of death of those who had been killed by mustard gas at Bari should be described as burns sustained in enemy action further increased the confusion and hampered investigations into this tragedy.

The Allies certainly had other ports, such as Naples for example, but Bari was their most suitable supply port. The injurious effects of the closure of the harbour at Bari was a further blow to the desperate attempts of the 5th Army and the 8th Army to push north. Then too, the loss of Bari as a supply port some weeks before the Allied landing at Anzio and Nettuno, which was to open the way to Rome, played a large part in enabling the Germans to hold up the Allies at both bridgeheads for longer than in any other campaign in the war.

On Monday 6 December 1943, after three days of fighting in which some of the units of the German 15th Panzer Grenadier Division were almost reduced to their last man, the 5th Army took the summit of Monte Camino.

By 8 December 1943 the Germans had managed to construct a new line in the Adriatic sector and re-establish the connection with the southern defences. The southern defences were centred around the plain where the Liri and Rapido join to become the Garigliano, which then flows into the Tyrrhenian Sea. The heights on either side of the lower Liri and behind the Rapido and Garigliano held the well dug-in positions of the Gustav Line.

Now, after two and a half months, the US 5th Army was at last

Lt.-Colonel Schlegel and the Abbot of Monte Cassino, Dom Gregorio Diamare.

within artillery range of the town of Cassino, and the fighting took on the character of a regular war of attrition.

On Wednesday 8 December 1943, Schlegel handed over to the Vatican representative all the treasures from the abbey of Monte Cassino, 120 lorry-loads altogether. Included among them were works by the great European masters, which had been evacuated to Monte Cassino from the state art gallery in Naples. Lt.-Colonel Schlegel again: '. . . Not one of the lorries nor any of the art-treasures were destroyed, and there was no damage to speak of. Everything valuable which could be moved was taken to safety.'

So ended the rescue of the art treasures – an operation practically unparalleled in history. Thanks to the spirited and courageous action of the Austrian many important monuments of western culture had been preserved for posterity.

On Tuesday 21 December 1943 the Canadian 1st Division began the assault on Ortona, a small port on the Adriatic coast. They met bitter resistance here and had to struggle for every inch of ground.

On Friday 24 December 1943 Generals Eisenhower and Montgomery were recalled to Great Britain for the invasion preparations. General Sir Henry Wilson was appointed Allied Commander-in-Chief Mediterranean Theatre; and the US 5th Army and British 8th Army were both placed under General Sir Harold Alexander as General Officer Commanding-in-Chief Allied Forces in Italy.

On Sunday 26 December 1943 the 2nd Moroccan Infantry Division and the 3rd Algerian Infantry Division of the French Expeditionary Corps (General Juin) went into action on the front as part of the 5th Army. These excellently equipped units, recruited from the mountain races of North Africa and led by French officers, proved a tough adversary for the Germans.

On Monday 27 December 1943 the Canadian 1st Division captured the port of Ortona; but here the 8th Army was forced to halt. It snowed and rained almost ceaselessly, the roads had turned to a morass, and

General Giraud (second from right), with General Juin (third from right), in conference with officers of the French Expeditionary Corps.

Moroccan troops of the French Expeditionary Corps file down a street near Colli. The colonial soldiers from Morocco and Algeria had a fine combat record.

on New Year's Eve another snowstorm raged in the mountains. When it cleared in the evening the villages and all forward positions were lying under a deep blanket of snow, with all road communications cut.

During early January the rumble of Allied guns was heard in Cassino for the first time. The surrounding villages were all evacuated, and on Tuesday 4 January 1944, the 5th Army made another attack on the approaches to the Gustav Line. The 132nd Grenadier Regiment of the 44th Infantry Division, the '*Hoch- und Deutschmeister*' (named after one of Prince Eugene's regiments), had the duty of defending the town of Cassino. After heavy losses earlier in the war, it was being replenished mainly by soldiers from the western regions of Poland, who scarcely spoke German but had been conscripted into the *Wehrmacht* as '*Volksdeutsche*' (ethnic Germans).

On Wednesday 12 January units of the French Expeditionary Corps (General Juin) broke through to the Gustav Line, reached Sant'Elia on 15 January and occupied Monte Santa Croce. American troops had taken Monte Trocchio by storm on the same day and so the Allies had now arrived at the whole length of the Gustav Line.

On Saturday 15 January shells fired by American artillery burst on the monastery for the first time and damaged the great fresco by Luca Giordano above the portal of the basilica. The monastery was now isolated; its sole inhabitants were the abbot and five monks, the secular priest, a deaf and dumb servant and three sick peasant families.

FIRST PHASE
17 January – 11 February

Failure on the Rapido

French Forces Approach the Rapido

Opposite: An observer of an American artillery regiment looks across at German positions on Monte Trocchio. The Allied censors have obliterated the divisional badge on his left arm before permitting the photograph to be released.

Monday 17 January 1944
The Times *reports:* American troops of the Fifth Army, advancing on Monte Trocchio, captured this important height before nightfall yesterday. To-day they have been consolidating their newly gained positions. Their attack was made in the face of a heavy concentration of artillery by the enemy, who had fortified his positions on this height very strongly with concrete gun emplacements and numerous strong-points. Monte Trocchio is the last height south of the Rome road before the Rapido Valley.

In the northern sector of the Fifth Army front General Juin's French troops have captured Cardito, on the mountain road which runs westward from Colli to Atina, roughly parallel with the Rome road, and pushing farther west have occupied Monte Croce. . . .

South of these positions the village of Vallerotonda was taken by French forces which moved forward from Monte Ferro and Monte Pagano and are now attacking along the mountain road from Acquafondata to San Elia. Yesterday these French troops had advanced to within two miles of San Elia, the strongly held village through which runs the River Rapido as it bends eastward after crossing the road north of Cassino.

Fifth Army Reaches the Rapido

Monday 17 January 1944
Allied Force Headquarters announces: Fifth Army troops continued their advance. Newly won positions on Monte Trocchio have been consolidated and forward troops have reached the River Rapido.

French troops in the hills near San Elia, unpacking their mules. Mule transport made the French the most effective mountain troops of the campaign.

Americans Cross the Rapido

Wednesday 19 January 1944

The Times *reports:* At one point north of Cassino the Americans crossed the river, but made no contact with the enemy until they were 300 yards beyond the other bank. Heavy defences were then met, and it seems that, having lost the high ground north of San Elia, the enemy has fallen back to the Gustav line.

Enemy Attack Repulsed

Friday 21 January 1944

German Supreme Command announces: . . . On the southern Italian front superior enemy forces attacked and after heavy fighting succeeded in breaking through south-west of Castelforte. In a methodical counter-attack they have been driven back to their initial positions. At a further breach north-west of Minturno fighting is still going on . . .

Allied Landings South of Rome

Sunday 23 January 1944

Allied Headquarters announces: In the large-scale amphibious operation in which British and American troops of the Fifth Army were landed south of Rome a substantial beachhead was seized. This beachhead has been widened and deepened.

The thrust seriously threatens enemy lines of communication leading south and east to the main battle line.

Along the main battle line the French attack to the west in the mountain sector is continuing against strong opposition.

American troops have enlarged their River Rapido bridgehead. Both they and British troops have repulsed enemy counter-attacks.

The landing at Anzio: British soldiers aboard amphibious DUKWs prepare to come ashore.

Anglo-American Landing at Nettuno

23 January 1944
German Supreme Command announces: . . . After heavy preliminary bombardment enemy forces made a renewed attack on our higher positions in the western sector of the southern Italian front. They were driven back with severe casualties. Enemy attempts to cross the Garigliano collapsed under our concentrated artillery fire. 500 men were taken prisoner. In the early hours of 22 January British and American troops landed either side of Nettuno on the coast of the Tyrrhenian Sea. Counter-measures are still in progress. The Luftwaffe attacked the enemy invasion fleet with great success, sinking four large landing craft totalling 12,000 gross register tons . . .

Port of Anzio Captured

Tuesday 25 January 1944
Allied Headquarters announces: The beach-head established south of Rome has been enlarged and strengthened, and the port of Anzio is in our hands. Our troops have advanced farther inland, but as yet have met no formidable enemy opposition.

On the southern Fifth Army front enemy counter-attacks have been repulsed. Advances were made by our troops at two points against determined enemy resistance.

The Situation in Rome

Wednesday 26 January 1944
Stefani's Agency reports: The proximity of the war zone, which up to now has hardly affected everyday life, has become distinctly noticeable during the last twenty-four hours. A 5 pm curfew has already been imposed, and food supplies are becoming perceptibly scarcer; the markets and food shops are especially short of fruit and vegetables. All the bridges are guarded by German sentries.

Advance Through Minefields

Wednesday 26 January 1944
Allied Force Headquarters announces: French troops of the Fifth Army are engaged in a bitter see-saw struggle with the enemy for possession of important heights several miles north-east of Cassino. In the Cassino sector American troops are advancing through minefields. In the northern beach-head British and American troops have continued to press forward against gradually increasing resistance.

Appian Way Shelled

Thursday 27 January 1944

The Times *reports:* The position here is that we are extending the bridgehead to gain elbow-room and the Germans are trying to contain us.

The Appian Way is under shellfire, but no troops are yet across it. The Germans hold Littoria, possibly with elements of the Hermann Göring Division, and their hurried arrival is indicated by the dropping of supplies by parachute. There are also signs of digging in on the central sector.

The Struggle at Anzio

Friday 28 January 1944

Radio Beromünster reports: During the past week, landing of British-American forces took place in central Italy behind the German front, at the small harbours of Anzio and Nettuno. General Alexander himself commanded these landing operations, which obviously came as a complete surprise to the enemy as not only was there no German resistance, but Allied units stumbled across a German battalion at rest and took it unawares. This landing ensued just as stubborn fighting between Kesselring's German units and General Clark's Americans (together with the French of General Juin) was raging on the Garigliano and at Cassino.

A battery of 155mm howitzers of the French Expeditionary Corps in action around Acquafondata, January 1944.

American troops dig in after landing at Anzio. The time spent in consolidating the beach-head was severely criticized by many observers.

All Attacks at Nettuno and Cassino Repulsed

Monday 31 January 1944

German Supreme Command announces: In southern Italy strong enemy infantry and armoured forces came up from the beach-head at Nettuno, attacking north and north-east. At the same time enemy attacks on the southern front greatly increased in intensity, particularly around Minturno and Cassino. The results of this mighty effort by the enemy were insignificant in terms of ground gained, but large in terms of their casualties.

Several raids into our main fortified zone were fought off by decisive counter-attacks. Fighting is still going on at other points. Over 900 men were taken prisoner by our troops.

Americans Breach German Defences

Tuesday 1 February 1944

The Times *reports:* American troops north of Cassino on the main Fifth Army front have, after three days hard fighting, penetrated the German defences across the River Rapido. Two important heights were captured on the road from Terelle to Cassino, and fierce fighting continues in this area.

The Americans surprised the enemy by their powerful well-timed breakthrough, as is indicated by their capturing in one village a 75mm anti-tank gun complete with its crew of 15 men. They succeeded in getting tanks across country in spite of much of the land being flooded through the enemy's diversion of the course of the Rapido.

Bloody Collapse of Enemy Attacks

Tuesday 1 February 1944
German Supreme Command announces: . . . In southern Italy fighting increased in intensity after the arrival of reinforcements on both sides. near Nettuno enemy forces continued their attacks in force towards the north and north-east. Their attempts to break through collapsed during bloody fighting. On the southern front enemy forces were restricted to localized attacks as a result of their heavy casualties on Monday . . .

The Village of Cairo Taken

Wednesday 2 February 1944
The Times *reports:* . . . the Fifth Army is exerting the strongest possible pressure on its southern front. Resistance in the village of Cairo, which had been enveloped, has been finally stifled. Cassino itself, one of the strongest places in the whole line of defence, has been imperilled by the turning movement from the north, and the enemy may be compelled to abandon it without the Americans having to resort to a frontal assault, which would probably be very costly.

It appears that the enemy intends to cling on to the Gustav line–or what is left of it–as long as possible, while the battle south of Rome is decided.

Heavy Casualties on Both Sides

Thursday 3 February 1944
German Supreme Command announces: . . . In southern Italy yesterday, at the beach-head of Nettuno, the enemy made some unsuccessful localized attacks against the northern front. Concentrated counter-attacks reduced yesterday's achievements by the enemy to nothing. On the southern front a bitter struggle is taking place for the Cassino massif. Control of the heights remains in German hands. Casualties on both sides are high . . .

Americans Near Cassino

Thursday 3 February 1944
The Times *reports:* The American crossing of the Rapido last week took place at a point about two miles north of Cassino, thanks largely to the clever work of the engineers. The Germans had closed the river sluices higher up, thus flooding the meadows through which the American tanks and infantry had to advance. The tanks were bogged and the infantry held up by mines.

Illingworth's cartoon for the Daily Mail late in January presented an overly optimistic picture of the Allied landings at Anzio. Although the Allies achieved some initial surprise the invasion forces were quickly contained within the Anzio–Nettuno beach-head.

Enemy Stronghold Threatened

Thursday 3 February 1944
Allied Headquarters announces: On both the Anzio and main fronts of the Fifth Army there has been hard fighting. The beach-head was enlarged in the face of stiff resistance, and counter-attacks were repulsed on the main front. French and American troops have moved so far through the mountains north of Cassino that this enemy stronghold is threatened seriously. Counter-attacks against the flank of our troops exploiting the break-through in this sector were thrown back. Eighth Army patrols were active.

Drama of Cassino Draws to a Close

Friday 4 February 1944
The Times *reports:* The drama of Cassino is drawing to a close. As the Americans extend their hold on the heights above the village of Cairo, and the French close in on Terelle, the German hold on the mountain mass which blocks the valley is gradually being prised open.

Grim House to House Struggle

Saturday 5 February 1944
The Times *reports:* The battle for Cassino on the main Fifth Army front is drawing to its close. American troops, supported by tanks, are in the outskirts of the town, and the struggle for this pivot of the Gustav line has become a grim and bitter fight from house to house among the desolate ruins that serve now the single purpose of desperate defence.

German Counter-Attacks Repulsed

Monday 7 February 1944
Allied Headquarters announces: On the main Fifth Army front hard fighting continues in the Cassino sector. Advances have been made north and west of the town. On the Anzio front American and British troops of the Fifth Army fought off strong counter-attacks, and took many prisoners.

After the optimism of late January, British opinion – and in particular Illingworth's cartoons – expressed much more realistic attitudes towards the possibilities of success in early February. Note that the main article on this page is by Basil Liddell Hart.

MONDAY, The Daily Mail, FEBRUARY 7, 1944.

WAR COMMENTARY

A new phase in Italy

by
CAPTAIN LIDDELL HART

A FURTHER week's continuation of the new two-pronged battle in Italy has tended to confirm the signs that were emerging last week-end. The landing at Nettuno, behind the enemy's flank, did not succeed in dislocating his hold on the main front, though it may have helped to loosen it and thus induce him to make another short withdrawal there.

The limited effect was apparently due to a deliberate limitation put upon the exploitation of this amphibious turning move in the early stages, when its surprise effect had created an admittedly big opportunity.

It is premature to criticise that decision; it must be left for the military historians to judge, when all the facts are available. What is important to appreciate is that the battle now developing forms a different kind of operation.

Two fronts

revert to the defensive for the time being. Observers draw a parallel between the bridgehead and Tobruk—which is not altogether a happy simile. But if the enemy is frustrated, and at the same time is led to press his attacks sufficiently to use up his strength, a better opportunity may come for a subsequent push on our side.

In concentrating so much of his strength here, Kesselring is probably relying on the cover-value of the 70-miles interval of hill-country backed by marshes which lie between the two limbs of the Fifth Army. At the same time, he seems to be pulling back from the Gustav Line to the next line in the rear.

Misleading

HE may calculate that the risk of reducing the interval between the two Allied forces will be compensated by the closer interconnection of his own, while a short withdrawal will also help to ease the pressure on his southern front.

It is in the light of these balancing factors that we have to gauge the progress achieved near Cassino by the Allied forces.

Wednesday's official announce-

THAT ROAD TO ROME —by Illingworth.

Allies Blocked at Cassino

Tuesday 8 February 1944

The Times *reports:* The grim struggle for Cassino, the key-point in the German defence of the road to Rome, is not yet over. American troops of the Fifth Army north of the town have pressed on beyond Monte Majola, and have captured three more heights to the west, thus threatening the main road, the Via Casilina, on that side of Cassino. Nearer the town itself Americans have advanced to within 100 yards of the crest of Monte Cassino, the 1,600ft.-high hill on which stands an ancient monastery. The capture of this height within a mile of the Rome road would further menace the Germans' supply route to Cassino.

Fierce and bitter fighting continues all round the town, and the enemy recaptured one hill about 500ft. west of the town during one violent counter-attack.

In the Anzio-Nettuno beach-head area the Germans are continuing their attack along both the British and American line of advance. Two miles north of Carroceto enemy infantry and tanks which were forming up to attack the British were dispersed by our artillery fire. Three miles west of Cisterna a strong enemy attack with infantry, supported by tanks, was launched against the Americans during the evening of Saturday and achieved some initial success, but in a fierce counter-attack the American forces later restored their positions.

Fierce Fighting Near Cassino

Wednesday 9 February 1944

Allied Headquarters announces: Advances were made by both British and American troops on the main Fifth Army front. Fierce fighting continues in and near Cassino. In the Fifth Army's Anzio beach-head the enemy continued to probe our positions.

Allies Spare Monastery

Thursday 10 February 1944

The Times *reports:* The Americans are still stuck within a few hundred yards of the monastery. Their guns are careful not to make it a target. The Army Command is mindful not only of the historical associations of the place, but of the precious manuscripts and art treasures from the University, library, and museums of Naples which are believed still to be stored there. The Germans trade on this discrimination and our men can see wireless aerials established on the roofs and telescopes at the windows.

On the afternoon of 17 January 1944 the British X Corps (Lt.-General McCreery) opened up with an intense bombardment of the positions held by the German 94th Infantry Division (Maj.-General Steinmetz). The first battle of Monte Cassino had begun.

At 9.00 pm the British divisions went into the attack across the lower Garigliano. At the same time a fighting force was to land in the Bay of Gaeta north of Minturno, behind the German lines. They were supported by artillery fire from the cruisers HMS *Orion* and HMS *Spartan* and five destroyers. Most of the landing craft lost their bearings, however, and the assault troops landed behind the British lines instead. This first battle of Cassino was more like an over-hasty resumption of the faltering advance than an offensive: the troops, who after weeks of heavy fighting were in urgent need of a rest, were simply given the order to push on, for General Alexander was determined to destroy any German units stationed in central Italy.

The men of X Corps forced their way across the Garigliano despite fierce German counter-attacks, and held the bridgehead which they had established outside Castelforte at the foot of Monte Faito.

German artillery in action in the central Italian countryside. It was the accurate fire of weapons such as this 15 cm gun which broke up so many of the early Allied attacks on Cassino.

The German XIV Panzer Corps faced a serious threat: imminent Allied invasion of the Liri valley and the collapse of the entire Cassino front. Lt.-General von Senger und Etterlin urgently requested Field-Marshal Kesselring to send up the reserves, the 29th Panzer Grenadier Division (Maj.-General Fries) and the 90th Panzer Grenadier Division (Colonel Baade). Only a speedy and decisive counter-attack could save the situation in the southern sector of the Cassino front. Kesselring ordered the 94th Infantry Division as well as the 29th and 90th Panzer Grenadier Divisions, under the general command of the I Parachute Corps (Air Chief Marshal Schlemm), into the threatened sector on the Garigliano. In the words of Lt.-General von Senger und Etterlin:

> 'After I had summed up the situation of the division under attack, I got into direct contact with the Commander-in-Chief of the Italian front, Field-Marshal Kesselring, and requested him to make the decision to place both divisions at my disposal, in order to prevent the enemy breaking through. I was aware that the High Command was faced with a momentous decision.
>
> 'With the deployment of both divisions the Commander-in-Chief would be robbing himself of his strategic reserves. But in my judgement of the situation on my front it was the only possible way to prevent the division on my right wing being thrust back from the sea and driven towards the north behind the endangered centre of the corps front, thus turning the whole system of defence upside down. After a short pause for reflection Field-Marshal Kesselring granted my request. The immediate danger of break-through by the enemy was averted. But the price was high.'

In the Cassino sector during the night of 17/18 January 1944 a company from the US 141st Regiment under First-Lieutenant Navarette was sent on a reconnaissance of the German line of defence on the opposite side of the Rapido. Navarette managed to penetrate 800m (850 yards) west of the Rapido. But when all his men had reached the opposite bank, the German machine-gun nests opened fire. Twenty minutes later almost all the Americans were dead or wounded. Only a few survivors were able to struggle back to their lines through the icy water. None of them succeeded in ascertaining where the German positions were.

At that time the key position on the entire Cassino front as well as the Monte Cassino and Monte Cairo massif was defended by the 44th Infantry Division, the '*Hoch- und Deutschmeister*' (Lt-General Franek). In this sector of the front the main defensive line of the Gustav line lay close to the course of the Rapido. When the snow is melting the Rapido, as its name indicates, becomes a torrent, flowing at 13 km/h (8 miles per hour). In the sector under attack it has vertical

German troops of the 715th Infantry Division march past on Elefant *self-propelled tank destroyer. The soldier on the left carries an MG42 machine-gun, one of the finest weapons of the war, combining reliability, accuracy and an extremely high rate of fire.*

banks at almost every point and the water is up to 3m (9 feet) deep. Thus, although scarcely 20m (22 yards) wide, the Rapido forms a formidable obstacle. The river crossing was to take place north and west of Sant'Angelo, a village which lies on high ground above the Rapido. But along the river bank and in the village itself the Germans had worked for weeks, building deeply echeloned positions safe against artillery attack.

The US infantrymen were issued with two types of boat for this operation: a clumsy wooden vessel which would transport up to twenty-four men but which was not manoeuvrable in the current, and a three-man rubber dinghy vulnerable to enemy fire. First the boats had to be brought by lorry to the advanced assembly points, which were out of sight of the enemy.

After forcing their way across the Rapido the US II Corps (Maj.-General G. Keyes) was to invade the Liri valley, while the outflanking movement already started by the French Expeditionary Corps was

A German artillery spotter, his binocular periscope camouflaged to break up its outline, makes a careful survey of the landscape.

continued through the mountains on the right flank. A British attack on the extreme left wing would support this operation.

Carrying the heavy, unwieldy boats in addition to weapons and equipment over the slippery paths of the flat, open approaches to the river, without making a sound, was no easy task in the pitch dark. The immediate objective of the attack across the Rapido – according to the orders received by the 36th (Texas) Division (Maj.-General Walker) – was the encircling of the village of Sant'Angelo, 8km (5 miles) south of Cassino, from both north and south. Maj.-General Walker's men were to press on to Pignataro and prepare the way for the US 1st Armoured Division to break through into the Liri valley.

On Wednesday 20 January the bombers of the US 12th Tactical Air Force attacked the positions and communications of the German 15th Panzer Grenadier Division (Maj.-General Rodt), as well as supply lines between Rome and the Garigliano front.

Meanwhile, that afternoon, the German 29th Panzer Grenadier Division (Maj.-General Fries) counter-attacked with an enveloping movement and drove back the British 56th Division (Maj.-General Templer) beyond Castelforte. The German attack came unexpectedly and just at the moment when the tired British troops were being regrouped and the British artillery was taking up new positions to give stronger support to its own assault units.

At 8.00 am on 20 January 1944 the assault companies of the 141st and 143rd Regiments began the painful march to the bank of the Rapido with their boats. The 142nd Regiment formed a reserve. The meadows between the assembly points and the river had been turned into a near-swamp because of artificial flooding and continual rain; in addition dense rising mist made orientation difficult. The terrain was open to heavy German artillery and mortar fire. Artillery fire shredded some of the white marking ribbons along the German mine-fields, so that in their search for cover the soldiers often found themselves in the middle of mine-fields which had only been partly cleared, and suffered heavy casualties.

The American infantry had no idea in which direction to advance, and worse still, the artillery behind them had no idea where their own troops were. Even the guides familiar with the ground got lost: one bridge-building unit was not found until hours later – a good 2km (1¼ miles) from the crossing place.

When the companies eventually reached the Rapido, their own artillery, which was supposed to pin down the Germans on the opposite bank, had to cease firing. Some boats, caught by artillery and machine-gun fire, sank as they were launched; some capsized and some were swept away as the infantry failed to control them.

Not until well after 9.00 pm did a few boat crews succeed in reaching the opposite bank. During the night engineers tried to construct an emergency bridge from the remains of the four bridges destroyed by mines and artillery bombardment, for reinforcements to be sent over to the other side.

It was eventually ready at 4.00 am: two companies even succeeded in traversing this footbridge, before it fell victim to German artillery fire. As dawn broke, all lines of communication to the troops on the other side, even by radio, were cut.

At daybreak on 21 January the American bridgehead and the crossing point were in full view of the Germans, and their tanks and self-propelled artillery proceeded to reduce the American bridgehead. In order to save his men the commanding officer of the 143rd Regiment requested permission to abandon his position, which was denied him. But before the orderly could reach him with the command he had retreated with his men on his own initiative.

The US 34th Infantry Division (Maj.-General Ryder) which was fighting north of Cassino had more luck: after crossing the Rapido it was able to hold out on the other side.

On Friday 21 January, at 5.00 am, the allied invasion fleet set sail from Naples harbour in the direction of Anzio and Nettuno. The warships, transports and landing craft, totalling 243 vessels, were under the command of Rear-Admiral Troubridge (RN) and Rear-Admiral Lowry (US Navy). This armada was carrying 50,000 assault troops and 5000 military vehicles, the forces which were to go into action as Operation 'Shingle', the landing of the US VI Corps (Maj.-General J. Lucas), behind German lines.

In the morning of 21 January Maj.-General Walker ordered the remnants of the 141st Regiment to cross the Rapido under cover of a smokescreen. Not until 6.30 pm did one of the battalions manage to set foot on the other side. Then, by means of a makeshift footbridge, another battalion of the 141st likewise gained the bridgehead.

At the same time, the 143rd Regiment, which in the southern sector had retreated across the river during the morning, failed in a second attempt to establish another bridgehead. The 141st Regiment was now reduced to forty men; 857 men were taken prisoner. The US 36th (Texas) Division had lost a total of 2066 men without achieving its objective.

After the failure on the Rapido, General Juin, commanding the French Expeditionary Corps, was ordered to change the direction of attack and first take Monte Belvedere with his troops. From there he was to turn south and join up with the Americans. This manoeuvre would allow the French to attack the German positions from the rear. In order to reach Monte Belvedere they had to cross the Rapido and

An American 13–26 medium bomber of the US 12th Air Force releases its load over German positions during the struggle to force the German defences.

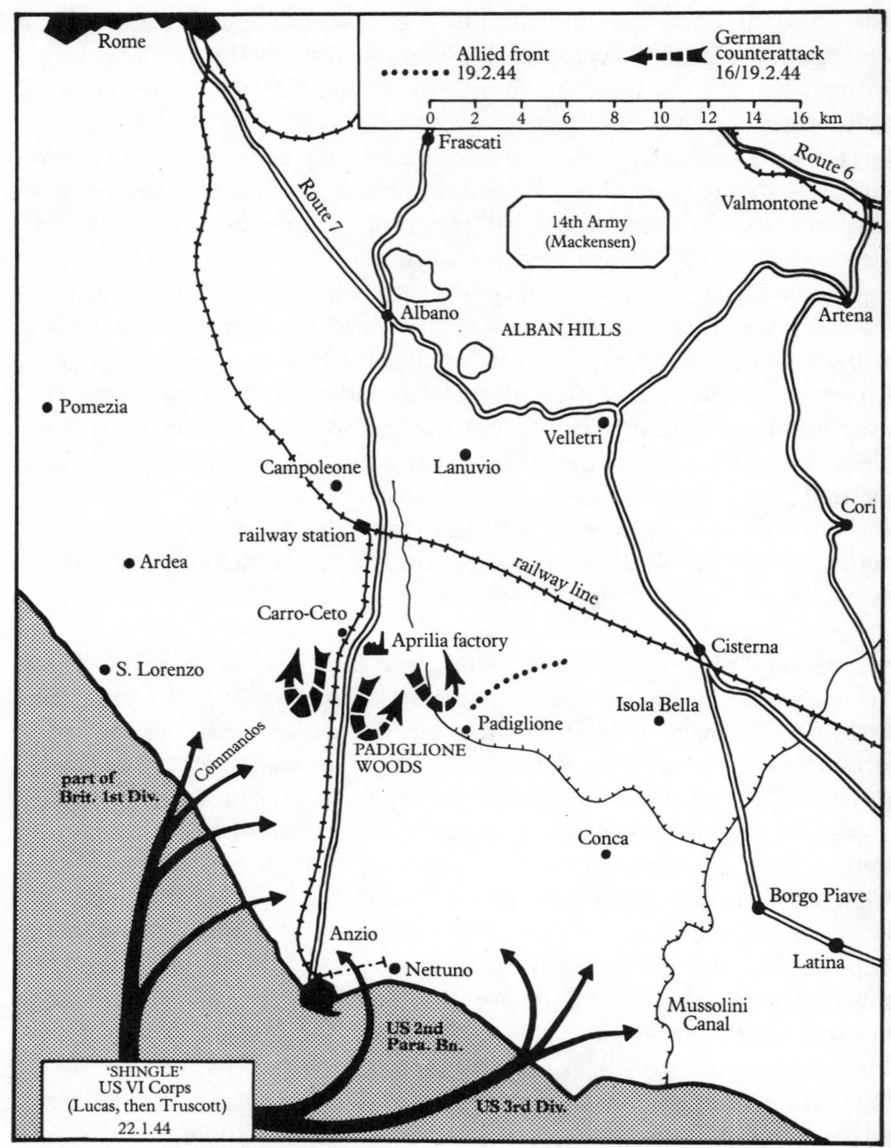

Operation 'Shingle', the Anzio landings.

Rio Secco rivers besides making two difficult mountain climbs and one descent, and all this under the eyes of the Germans who were lying in wait on the summits of the surrounding mountains. In the valleys again, German mortars and other artillery were trained on all the ravines, passes and footpaths. Monte Belvedere is a mountain over 700m (2300 feet) high, furrowed by rock fissures and completely treeless. In addition, the approach paths were still crumbling and slippery from rain and snow. On the summit of Monte Belvedere the Germans had entrenched themselves in machine-gun nests and bunkers protected by mines and barbed-wire.

During the night of 22 January 1944 the 2nd Battalion of the US 143rd Regiment was able to push 400m (440 yards) west, but then the attack faltered and the German 129th Panzer Grenadier Regiment with artillery support forced the Americans back over the river again, taking almost 500 prisoners. As already mentioned, however, the attacks along the Garigliano were intended to pin the German reserves on this front; and in this they were successful.

On 22 January 1944 at 2.00 am the US VI Corps (Maj.-General Lucas), composed of the British 1st and US 3rd Divisions, landed at Anzio, 36km (22 miles) from Rome. The beaches at Anzio and the fishing-port of Nettuno were ideal for this operation. A broad plain rose gently and uninterruptedly up to the Alban Hills, and on the right flank of the beach-head lay a mighty tank ditch, the 'Mussolini Canal'. After crossing the Alban Hills the Allied plan was to cut Highways 6 and 7, along which all German supplies south were carried. Allied air force commanders were sure that the Germans could be prevented from bringing up reinforcements by bombing their communications; but in this their optimism was misplaced.

At the time of the landing, the Germans had just two infantry battalions and some light coastal batteries available for defence in the area. The first German troops the Allied forces ran into that night were 200 men sent there to recover from the heavy fighting on the Cassino front. They were surprised in their sleep and taken prisoner.

The landing, 96km (60 miles) behind the German Gustav Line, was accomplished with astonishingly few casualties: thirteen dead, ninety-seven wounded and forty-four missing. But what Maj.-General Lucas failed to realize was that Rome lay practically undefended before him, and could have been taken by a surprise attack. Instead of taking advantage of surprise and advancing along the highway to Rome, he confined himself to the consolidation of the beach-head and the disembarkation of vehicles and equipment, in defiance of Napoleon's maxim, '*activité, activité, vitesse*'.

In the morning of 22 January the British Guards Brigade made a cautious thrust from the beach-head towards Campoleone, and the US 3rd Division moved towards Cisterna. General Alexander reported on this move to Churchill, 'We appear to have got complete surprise. I have stressed the importance of strong-hitting, mobile patrols being boldly pushed out to gain contact with the enemy, but so far have not received reports of their activities.' The landing at Anzio-Nettuno promised to provide the means of shortening the campaign. It was also hoped that the operation to the rear of the Gustav Line would mirror this success.

That same day, the 90th Panzer Grenadier Division (Colonel Baade) went into action on the Cassino front. Hampered by attacks from

E.G. Baade, commander of the 90th Panzer Grenadier Division, following his promotion to general rank.

Moroccan goumiers *on their way up to the mountain front; with 'meat on the hoof' accompanying them.*

fighter-bombers the division could not reach the battle-field as a single force, but some of its units took part in defensive fighting with the 94th Infantry Division (Maj.-General Steinmetz) in the southern sector.

By midnight on 22 January about 36,000 men and 3100 vehicles had been landed at Anzio. The heavy German He 177 bombers of II *Gruppe** of *Kampfgeschwader* 40 and the Do 217s of *Kampfgeschwader* 100 made unsuccessful attempts to prevent the build-up by attacking with radio-controlled glider bombs (the FX 1400 and Hs 293 models). The American destroyers *Woolsey*, *Frederick C. Davis* and *Herbert C. Jones* tried to jam the remote control of the glider bombs by sending out strong radio signals themselves and their efforts ensured that only some of the bombs reached their targets. On Sunday 23 January the British destroyer *Jervis* was the first ship to be hit by a radio-guided Hs 293 bomb. In spite of serious damage she was able to make for Naples under her own steam.

That same evening both the Allied divisions with their special units – among them two British Commandos, US Rangers and para-troops – and an enormous quantity of supplies were ashore in full strength. The fortification of the bridgehead at Anzio-Nettuno was making progress; but, as Churchill remarked, the opportunity of a break-out had disappeared.

By Monday 24 January 1944, then, 50,000 men had already landed at Anzio-Nettuno, yet now Maj.-General Lucas decided to wait for his heavy artillery and tanks. He ordered the troops to make the bridge-head secure and to dig themselves in.

The situation of the Germans was still perilous, but Field-Marshal Kesselring had reacted with the utmost speed and skill. Although his reserves were already committed to the heavy fighting on the Cassino front he gathered together (even from there) whatever units could be spared, and on 24 January sent an assault force of about two divisions to attack the Allied bridgehead, which was roughly 17km (11 miles) deep and 24km (15 miles) wide. He then sent sections of the 3rd Parachute Regiment to attack the bridgehead. The German 14th Army (Colonel-General von Mackensen) was to blockade the US VI Corps in its beach-head until enough troops had been assembled for a counter-attack. Hitler: 'If we manage to polish off that business down there, there will be no further landings.'

The Allied air forces now aimed at the German supply lines, so that movement only became possible at night, and from dawn till dusk artillery spotter planes circled untiringly over the front line. The Allies, however, had over-estimated the effect of their air attacks. They could certainly hinder troop movements but not eliminate them altogether. Nine divisions were transferred from French Provence and Austrian Carinthia and rushed to the battle area. Churchill was very

*See note page 53.

German paratroops move up to the Anzio front in a variety of transport, from motor-cycle sidecars to SdKfz 232 armoured cars.

impressed by the seeming ease with which the Germans moved up reinforcements and the rapidity with which they adjusted the gaps they had to make on the southern front.

On 24 January at 10.00 pm the 3rd Algerian Infantry Division (Maj.-General de Goislard de Monsabert) of the French Expeditionary Corps attacked on the Cassino front to pin down the troops there. Their first targets were Monte Belvedere, Colle Abate and the village of Terelle, over 900m (3000 feet) up on the northern slope of Monte Cairo. In the mountainous terrain north of Monte Cassino they were to envelop the German Cassino front from the rear. While the US 34th Division was fighting in the marshy Rapido valley, the French Corps attacked the Germans from the flank a few kilometres further north.

First of all, a battalion of Tunisian infantry attempted to storm Monte Cifalco which commanded the area. The attempt failed however, in the face of vigorous resistance by the German 5th Mountain Division. Then, after they had overcome barbed-wire entanglements and mine-fields, the other battalions of the Tunisian 4th Rifle Regiment crossed the Rapido. Climbing the steep slopes of

Soldiers of the 4th Moroccan Division halt their vehicles near Cassino. They were largely equipped from American sources.

Monte Belvedere, held by grenadiers of the 44th Infantry Division, the '*Hoch- und Deutschmeister*', the Tunisians came under heavy German artillery fire, directed by the observers on Monte Cifalco.

At first the French troops had considerable success but they were held up by the 90th Panzer Grenadier Division (Colonel Baade) and sections of the 71st Infantry Division (Maj.-General Raapke) positioned here. Further attempts by the US 34th Division to capture Monte Cassino also came to grief.

In the morning of 25 January Lt.-General Clark ordered the 34th Infantry Division, to storm the town of Cassino from the north. They were to traverse the 3km (2 miles) wide marshy area (which had been created by exploding a dam on the upper reaches of the Rapido), then ford the icy river and make a frontal attack on Monte Cassino. The first thrust was to be made by the 133rd Regiment, which was to capture two rocky spurs and the Italian barracks at the foot of the mountain. Afterwards the 168th Regiment was detailed to take Monte Castellone, the Colle Sant'Angelo and the Albaneta farm. The 135th Regiment was to proceed along the road parallel to the Rapido and the mountains and take the town of Cassino, 2.5km (1.5 miles) away. The task facing the American units was truly formidable: on the other side of the river the defences of the Gustav Line began and a cliff rose almost vertically. Disaster struck almost as soon as the attack got under way: the tanks stuck fast in the muddy ground and the 135th Regiment were caught in a mine-field after covering only 200m (220 yards). The other units did reach the Rapido but were halted by heavy infantry fire from the old Italian barracks. On the afternoon of 25 January, however, the tirailleurs of the Tunisian 4th Rifle Regiment succeeded in hoisting a *tricolore* on Monte Belvedere.

On that day the German 14th Army (Colonel-General von Mackensen) took over the task of sealing off the beach-head at Anzio-Nettuno, after the Germans in their turn had failed since 22 January to take advantage of the Allied moment of weakness by making a decisive counter-thrust.

During the night of 25 January the US 34th Division (Maj.-General Ryder) again ventured across the Rapido. With strong artillery support the 133rd Infantry Regiment succeeded in getting three battalions across the river near the old Italian barracks. After the German 134th Grenadier Regiment counter-attacked however, the Americans had to retreat across the Rapido again as they had no tank support. The width of the front in the Cassino sector was much too narrow for armour to manoeuvre effectively, and the concentrated German artillery fire often decimated tanks in the assembly areas.

On the morning of 26 January 1944 the 133rd Regiment made renewed attacks in the Cassino sector – again without tank support. Each battalion involved reported over 100 casualties. The sending-in of the 135th Regiment north of Cassino town brought no success either. Only a single company succeeded in crossing the Rapido; the other units had to pull back in the face of heavy German defensive fire. And an attack immediately afterwards by the 100th 'Nisei' Battalion (a unit composed of Americans of Japanese descent) foundered in the wet ground and mine-fields.

The French Expeditionary Corps still pushed on, in spite of these American setbacks; on the 26th, theTunisian 2nd Battalion captured Colle Abate and the important Point 862 north-east of it. They were already nearing their target of Terelle. Now, however, their supply line was cut and they began to run out of ammunition and rations. The German Panzer grenadiers counter-attacked, storming towards Point 862 and Colle Abate, as the Tunisians desperately defended themselves with knives and bayonets.

At dawn on 27 January the US 168th Infantry Regiment attempted to extend the small bridgehead held by the 133rd Regiment. This time the American tanks succeeded in making their way to the river, and by 9.30 am four Sherman tanks managed to cross to the other side of the Rapido. The following tanks, however, stuck fast in the mud and blocked the way. Towards mid-day the Germans destroyed the four tanks which had crossed the river. A company which had advanced along the road to Cassino town during the night was also driven back.

General Clark discusses a tactical problem with his staff.

There was a further German success when the Panzer grenadiers managed to win back Colle Abate, but the Tunisians continued to defend Monte Belvedere with grim resolution, in spite of the furious counter-attacks.

At Anzio, five days after the landing, the US 3rd Division was still in the beach-head south of Cisterna, and the British Guards Brigade, which had made some progress, was still about 3km (2 miles) outside Campoleone. The exploitation of the Anzio landing could now be said to have failed. The attacks on Cisterna and Campoleone had already been driven back by the German reinforcements; moreover the bridgehead now came under fire and German railway-mounted guns smashed the harbour of Nettuno to pieces. The Anzio-Nettuno failure was a particular disappointment for Winston Churchill, who had looked on the Italian campaign as having such great possibilities for rapid success.

When it became clear how strong the German defence in the Cassino sector was, General Alexander decided to transfer some divisions from the British 8th Army to reinforce the 5th Army. From the 2nd New

An immobilized Tiger tank is investigated by German maintenance troops during the struggle for the Anzio beach-head. The influence of Allied air power is shown by the extensive camouflage on the armoured vehicles.

Zealand Division and the 4th Indian Division, both currently engaged in the Adriatic sector, he formed the New Zealand II Corps under Lt.-General Sir Bernard Freyberg. These élite formations had already distinguished themselves in North Africa and were among the best troops of the Commonwealth.

On Friday 28 January the 90th Panzer Grenadier Division took over from the 44th Infantry Division the sector on both sides of Terelle as far as the Secco valley, and including the whole of the Cassino sector. And on the same day the Tunisians on Monte Belvedere were at last relieved by the Algerian 7th Rifle Regiment. Between Anzio and Nettuno Maj.-General Lucas' troops had gained an area of ground about 15km (9 miles) wide, which was just big enough to eliminate the effect of the German field artillery on the landing beach and the harbour of the fishing town of Anzio.

On Saturday 29 January 1944, after US engineers had constructed tank roads on the approaches to Cassino town, stronger armoured forces advanced. With their support the US infantry reached Points 56 and 213. As darkness fell both hills were captured. At the same time the Algerian 7th Rifle Regiment attacked Colle Abate and Point 862.

At Anzio the German II *Gruppe** of *Kampfgeschwader* 100 attacked the British anti-aircraft cruiser *Spartan*, lying at anchor near the coast, and the freighter *Samuel Huntington* (7181 gross register tons). At 7.05 pm an Hs 293 hit the *Spartan* which shortly afterwards heeled over and sank. Almost simultaneously an Hs 293 set the *Samuel Huntington* on fire. At 3.00 am the following morning, the freighter exploded when flames reached its cargo of ammunition and fuel.

On Sunday 30 January the US 168th Infantry Regiment succeeded in crossing the Rapido and in the evening captured Cairo village at the foot of Monte Cairo. The staff officers of the 1st Battalion of the 131st Grenadier Regiment were taken prisoner.

On the same day General Lucas, who now had four divisions in the beach-head, decided to enlarge his sphere of operations. The US 3rd Division (Maj.-General Truscott) attacked Cisterna after a heavy preliminary bombardment, but was driven back with many casualties, and of two US Ranger battalions which had been cut off by the Germans only six men regained their own lines. Similarly, at Campoleone the US 1st Armoured Division was halted by mine-fields and tough German resistance. There was still no link between the US VI Corps which had landed at Anzio and the US 5th Army fighting outside Cassino. Maj.-General Truscott: 'One must admit, I think, that the original strategic conception erred in two respects: over-estimating the effect which the landings would have upon the German High Command; and underrating the German capacity for countering this move.'

*See note page 53

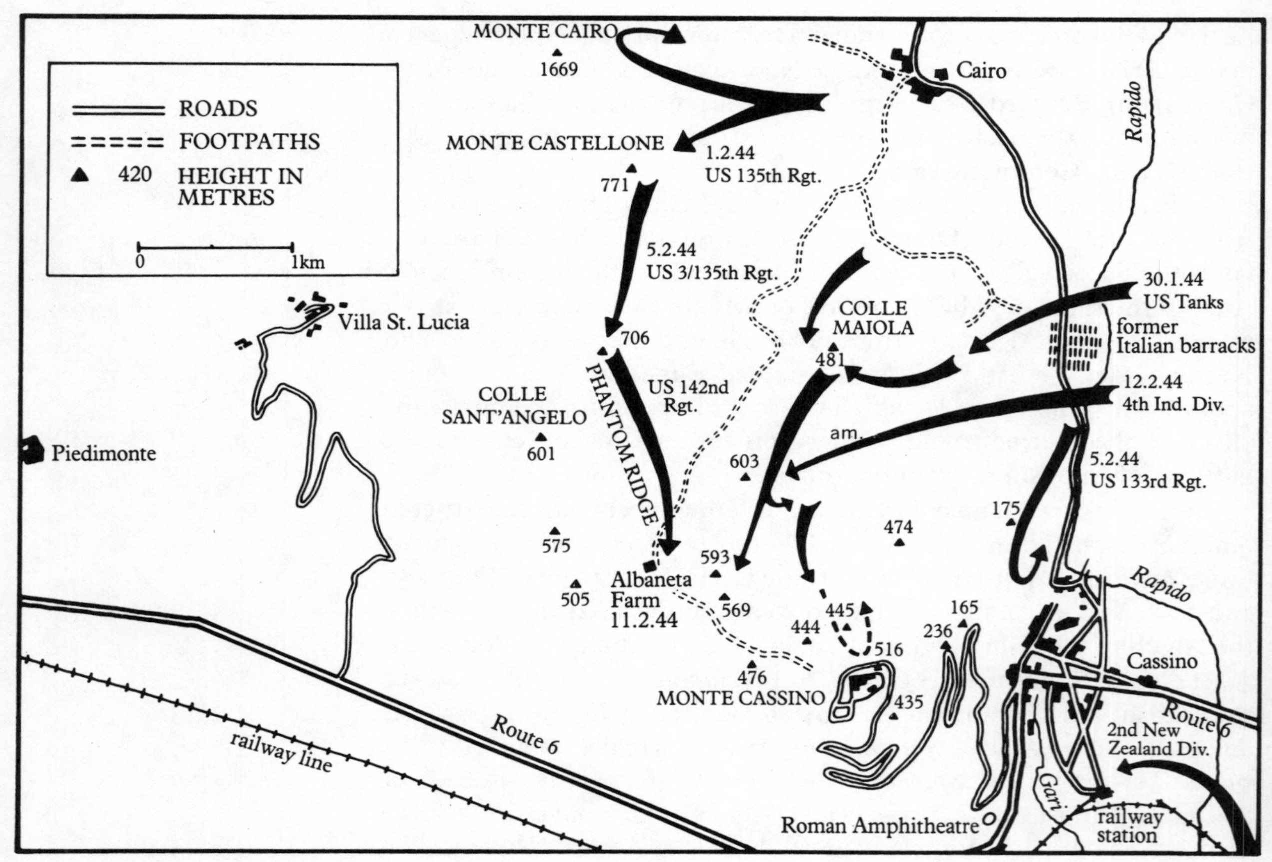

The initial American attacks on Cassino, and the New Zealand advance to the station.

The invasion forces had in the meantime been increased to 70,000 men and 356 tanks but the Anzio-Nettuno bridgehead had been sealed off by strong German forces. Five German divisions – although without air superiority – were facing three-and-a-half Allied divisions. General Patton, when visiting Lucas, had told him, '. . . you can't get out of this alive. Of course, you might be badly wounded. No-one ever blames a *wounded* general.'

In thick fog at daybreak on 1 February an attack by three regiments of the 34th Division started out from the ground already gained at Cairo north of Cassino town. The 168th Infantry Regiment was to capture Monte Calvario, Point 593, the tactical centre of the Monte Cassino massif. The 135th and 142nd Regiments advanced towards the other commanding heights, Monte Castellone and Colle Sant'Angelo. They captured Monte Castellone and Colle Maiola in turn. But the Colle Abate and Point 862 again fell to the German Panzer grenadiers after a furious assault.

On Wednesday 2nd February the 133rd Infantry Regiment pushed on in thick fog to within 3km (2 miles) of Highway 6, the Via Casilina.

An American soldier of the US 3rd Division surrenders to the German forces at Anzio. In the foreground is a German 3.7 cm anti-aircraft gun mounted on a 5 ton half-track.

After capturing the old Italian barracks the Americans assaulted the northern part of Cassino and Rocca Janula, Point 193. Reinforced by the US 760th Armoured Battalion, the infantry stormed the first houses on the northern edge of the town. In bitter hand-to-hand street-fighting the soldiers of the German 211th Grenadier Regiment were driven back almost 1000m (¾ mile) to the north.

On Thursday 3 February, however, the 135th and 168th Infantry Regiments were still only 3km (2 miles) north of the Via Casilina. The 133rd Infantry Regiment, although also successful in taking Point 175 and capturing a few houses on the outskirts, did not manage to penetrate further into Cassino in spite of heavy artillery support. At the same time, German paratroops were sent into the Cassino sector – the *Kampfgruppe* Schulz, the 1st Parachute Regiment with its machine-gun battalion, and the 3rd Battalion of the 3rd Parachute Regiment. These soldiers would soon prove themselves to be tough and skilful opponents in mountain warfare, for whom the Americans had a suitable name: the 'green devils'.

The German counter-attack now began at Nettuno. Units of the

Known by the Allies as the 'Anzio Express' this German 28 cm railway gun is prepared for action.

14th Army (Colonel-General von Mackensen) drove the British troops back to Aprilia and Carroceto, and halted the Americans south of Campoleone. German railway-mounted guns, nicknamed the 'Anzio Express' by Allied soldiers, opened fire on the harbour of Anzio and the transport ships; the landing beaches became targets for the German medium artillery.

On Friday 4 February the US 135th Infantry Regiment captured Colle Sant'Angelo in the Cassino sector, but was driven back again shortly afterwards. The 168th Infantry Regiment did, however, reach Monte Calvario (Point 593). The New Zealand II Corps (Lt.-General Freyberg) had now been officially formed, and the British 78th Division was assigned to it. Freyberg's first task was to take advantage of the expected American breakthrough by capturing Cassino town and Monastery Hill, entering the Liri valley and blocking Highway 6. The Americans did seem to be making progress: on Saturday 5 February an assault detachment of the 135th Infantry Regiment succeeded in advancing as far as the monastery wall of Monte Cassino. But it was not until the middle of May that Allied soldiers were again to come so close to the monastery.

In the bridgehead at Anzio there were now 18,000 vehicles,

A British artillery observer at his post in the front line of the Anzio beach-head.

including tanks, and 70,000 men. Churchill asked in amazement, 'How many of our men are driving or looking after 18,000 vehicles in this narrow space? We must have a great superiority of chauffeurs. I am shocked that the enemy has more infantry than we.'

During the night of 5 February the 168th Infantry Regiment was ordered to attack Monte Cassino from the north, from Point 445. But in a deep gully on the north face of Monastery Hill the Americans ran into machine-gun crossfire and had to retreat.

On Sunday 6 February the Polish General Anders arrived in Naples to establish contact with General Leese, Commander-in-Chief of the British 8th Army, to whom the Polish troops were to be attached. On the same day the 3rd Battalion of the US 135th Infantry Regiment took Point 593, Monte Calvario. This was the key to Monte Cassino, as it looked down over the whole town. The Germans were still holding out on the last heights above the Via Casilina, but once the Americans had captured these heights, they would then be able to control Cassino.

On Monday 7 February the 361st Regiment of the 90th Panzer Grenadier Division (Lt.-General* Baade) made a counter-attack on Point 593, captured the previous day by the US 135th Regiment. Sustaining heavy casualties, it wrested the hill from the Americans;

*Promoted on 1 February 1944.

Monte Cassino: A 15 cm howitzer of a German artillery battery is reloaded. At certain times the fighting in this sector degenerated into an artillery duel, as the infantry could make no progress.

but by Wednesday 9 February, only two days later, Monte Calvario was back in American hands. The Machine-Gun Battalion of the 1st Parachute Division, attached to *Kampfgruppe* Schulz, now took over the immediate defence of Monte Cassino, from Rocca Janula up to Monte Calvario. The 3rd Battalion of the 3rd Parachute Regiment was assigned to Point 593, and the 1st Parachute Regiment held the north slopes as far as Monte Castellone. At daybreak on 10 February the paratroopers of the 3rd Battalion – taking the American advance posts unawares – stormed the western slope of Monte Calvario, took it in a *coup de main* and scattered the Americans once more. Point 593 remained in German hands until the middle of May 1944.

10 February also saw German successes on the Anzio front. In a counter-attack the 1st Parachute Division and the LXXVI Panzer Corps drove the British out of Carroceto and the agricultural research station at Aprilia. Field-Marshal Kesselring pressed ahead with plans for a speedy and decisive counter-offensive. He wished to seal off the beach-head and to prevent the Allies from recovering their balance.

On Friday 11 February the Americans made a final attempt to capture Monte Calvario and Monte Cassino by frontal assault. After a long preliminary bombardment the 36th (Texas) Division (Maj.-General Walker) was to take Massa Albaneta and Monte Calvario, and the 34th Division (Maj.-General Ryder) was to take Monastery Hill from the north. Shortly before the attack began, however, a severe blizzard blew up, blotting out visibility for the Allied artillery observers and making support for the advancing infantry impossible. The German paratroopers, crouched in dug-outs, shell-holes and machine-gun nests, waited for the enemy. The 142nd Infantry Regiment was wiped out on the slopes of Monte Calvario; the 141st Infantry Regiment was decimated before it reached Albaneta. Wave after wave of attacking infantry collapsed before the German positions.

In the evening of 11 February 1944 the US II Corps gave up the fight for Monte Cassino. On average, its battalions now numbered scarcely 100 men. The corps had to be relieved and replaced by a fresh one; and so ended the first battle of Monte Cassino. On both sides, the attacking and defending forces were exhausted. The attack on Monastery Hill from Monte Calvario (Point 593) brought the Allies much valuable, though dearly won, experience; but many of the lessons were to be ignored in the succeeding battles. The only positive result of the first battle, apart from some successes north of Cassino, lay in the pinning down of German reserves and the prevention of their deployment at Anzio-Nettuno. The first battle of Monte Cassino was, therefore, a defensive victory for the Germans, although they too had paid a high price.

SECOND PHASE
12 February – 19 February

The Destruction of the Monastery

Germans on Road to Abbey

Friday 11 February 1944
The Times *reports:* German machine-gunners were known to be manning the road to the abbey of Monte Cassino, and men of the Fifth Army, groping their way up the slopes, have seen German machine-guns along the abbey walls.

Throughout the heavy allied bombardment of Cassino scrupulous care has been taken to avoid the monastery, which is situated on a crag 1,600ft. in height to the left of the town, overlooking the entire Cassino Valley.

Joining Forces

Saturday 12 February 1944
General Mark Clark to 5th Army: Men of the Fifth Army are fighting valiantly in important battles on two fronts. On January 22 our troops swarmed ashore at Anzio, just south of Rome, and swiftly captured a large area in the German flank and rear, and established a firm beach-head. As a result of our successful operation in the Rome area the enemy was forced to withdraw large numbers of troops from the Cassino and Garigliano front.

The next step in the successful operations which we have just commenced is for our two forces to join hands in a victorious march into Rome and to the north.

Warning Leaflets

Sunday 13 February 1944
The Times *reports:* Warning leaflets were to-day dropped by shell

Opposite: A German paratrooper, mainstay of the tenacious defence put up by the German forces around Cassino.

within Monte Cassino Abbey. The leaflets said:-

Italian friends, beware: we have until now been especially careful to avoid shelling Monte Cassino Monastery. The Germans know how to benefit from this. But now the fighting has swept closer and closer to its sacred precincts.

The time has come when we must train our guns on the monastery itself. We give you warning that you may save yourselves. We warn you urgently: leave the monastery. Leave it at once. Respect this warning. It is for your benefit. – Fifth Army.

Fantastic Input of Material by the Americans

Monday 14 February 1944
The German News Bureau reports: The situation on the Italian front in the last twenty-four hours has been dominated by the battle for Cassino, which is continuing with the utmost ferocity. Compared to this, fighting in the other sectors, even in the beach-head of Nettuno, has been insignificant. Supported by a fantastic input of material strong American units formed up on Sunday and this morning for an attack on the town of Cassino.

Stubborn Resistance on Monte Cassino

Monday 14 February 1944
The Times *reports:* On the main Fifth Army front the battle for Cassino pursues its bitter course. Two miles west of the town the Americans have captured a hill about 1,500ft. high and have repulsed a fierce counter-attack in which the enemy tried to recover it.

On Monte Cassino, known to the Army as Abbey Hill, above the town, enemy resistance is still extremely stubborn. It is disclosed today that the Vatican authorities had asked that the monastery at the crest of the hill, the cradle of the Benedictine order, should be spared. The allies have complied with the request as far as possible, but the Germans are using the monastery as a fortress, its large buildings and massive walls forming an important part of their defences dominating the road to Rome below. The monastery has not hitherto been a target for the allies' guns or bombers.

Benedictine Abbey in Flames

Sunday 15 February 1944
The German News Bureau reports: According to information, the Benedictine Abbey of Cassino has been in flames since the American attack this morning. As there were no German troops in the monastery or its vicinity at the time of the bombardment, there was no-one

available to fight the fire, and the venerable building could not be saved. In view of the complete destruction of the abbey, the repeated declarations by German High Command that the parent monastery of the Benedictine Order was to be eliminated from the sphere of military operations would seem to have lost any relevance.

Destruction of the Monastery; an Act of Revenge

Sunday 15 February 1944
The International Information Bureau reports: During the morning thirty American bombers attacked the venerable Benedictine Abbey of Cassino with large high-explosive bombs, which caused extensive damage to the monastery buildings. In order to invest this deed with a semblance of justification the Americans had previously dropped leaflets over the abbey and the ruins of Cassino town, in which they repeatedly asserted that the monastery had been converted by the German troops into all kinds of military defence works. In this respect the German authorities have again confirmed that the entire abbey and an extensive surrounding area had been barred to all military traffic. The world-famous monastery library was saved and brought to Rome a few months ago by troops of the German Luftwaffe. It was then handed over to the papal authorities in the Vatican, and since the

An American observer looks across at enemy positions.

evacuation of the library no German soldier has entered the monastery grounds. The only approach to Monte Cassino has been guarded by a German military policeman who prohibits any unauthorized person from entering the monastery. The destruction of the monastery of Cassino is an act of revenge by the Americans, whose attacks on the town of Cassino have failed again and again in the face of an obstinate German defence.

The Monastery Bombed

Wednesday 16 February 1944

The Times *reports:* The allied command's decision, carefully deliberated and most reluctantly adopted, to bomb the abbey at Monte Cassino was put into execution. . . . From 9.15 am onwards Fortresses, Mitchells, and Marauders, a squadron at a time, showered high explosives on the abbey hill every 20 minutes or so. . . . This two-hour bombardment of the abbey had been accompanied by a general assault of the allied artillery on the German position in and around Cassino and far back in the Liri valley. The rumbling of the guns near and far was unceasing. Shells were bursting in Cassino town and on the slopes above it. Others were falling on the ridge well behind the abbey.

British artillery engage enemy targets in the hills around Monte Cassino. The British Army relied heavily upon its artillery. Germans had a great respect for the ability of the British gunners.

The abbey at Monte Cassino under bombardment by American bombers. The bombing of the 13th century monastery was the most controversial decision of the campaign.

Protection of Historic Monuments

Wednesday 16 February 1944

The Times *reports:* As an indication of the reluctance with which the allied command ordered the bombing of the Benedictine abbey at Cassino, President Roosevelt read at his press conference to-day two orders issued by General Eisenhower on December 29 last concerning the protection of historic monuments.

The first order said that such monuments in Italy must be respected so far as the war allowed, but if commanders had to choose between destroying a famous building and sacrificing men, then lives counted infinitely more and the buildings must go. Nothing could stand against the argument of military necessity, but that should not be confused with military or even personal convenience, and he did not want the term 'military necessity' to cloak slackness or indifference. The second order provided for historic buildings to be clearly marked and protected by guards, if necessary, and forbade the occupation of historic buildings, even of secondary importance, if alternative accommodation was available.

German Defences Shattered

Thursday 17 February 1944
The Times *reports:* The bombing of the abbey of Monte Cassino has shattered the Germans' strongest defence of the road to Rome and of Cassino itself. By the late afternoon yesterday our artillery was shelling the remaining enemy positions on Monte Cassino, but there is no news at head-quarters of our troops having advanced across the last few hundred yards to the crest of the hill. It is now confirmed that we hold roughly one-third of the town of Cassino. Allied air force reconnaissance photographs are reported to show the complete destruction of the abbey.

Knee-Deep in Mud

Thursday 17 February 1944
Völkischer Beobachter *reports:* Heavy rain has covered the roads and paths skirting the Pontine marshes in the Nettuno beach-head with a soapy layer of clay. In the fox-holes and shell craters muddy water gurgles and sucks. In places, the grenadiers wade knee-deep in glutinous filth. This weather was all that was missing in the inferno in and around Aprilia. At every impact brown fountains of earth gush high into the sky. Large fragments of stone whirl through the air after shattering explosions, and above the main fighting line, like a menacing fist, trails of mist and powder clouds join with the plumes of smoke from the smouldering fires in bombed houses in a thunderous roar. The Fury of mechanized warfare rides over the land. Even when the cannons' mouths fall silent for a spell and Life anxiously draws breath again amidst the enormous expanse of ruin, infantry weapons thunder out over the positions and fast bombers protected by agile fighter escorts leave milky vapour trails behind them.

Hard Fighting North-West of Abbey

Friday 18 February 1944
Allied Headquarters announces: Heavy enemy attacks on the Anzio beach-head positions have been beaten off by British and American troops of the Fifth Army. On the main Fifth Army front there was hard fighting around a height north-west of the Cassino Abbey. Severe weather on the Eighth Army front prevented large scale activity.

First Phase of New Attack Over

Saturday 19 February 1944
The Times *reports:* The first phase of the new attack on Cassino, with the help of the Indian and New Zealand units, is over. It resulted in the

capture of two heights, which was necessary for successful operations against Monastery Hill. The first, known as Point 596, is a commanding ridge overlooking the abbey across a fold in the mountain from a distance of about a mile. The second is a shoulder of the same ridge nearer the abbey but lower.

An Allied soldier attempts to dig out a 4.5 inch field-gun from the thick mud which greatly hampered Allied operations in the low lying areas to the south of Cassino.

Position Unchanged in Cassino

Saturday 19 February 1944

The Times *reports:* On the main Fifth Army front the position remained unchanged in Cassino. Beyond the town in the area of Monte Albaneta, our forces captured a peak which they were later compelled to abandon after a heavy enemy counter-attack.

General Alexander, who had to confirm the decision to bomb the abbey. Although a number of senior officers opposed such a course of action, he was swayed by Freyberg's insistence that the Abbey be destroyed.

THE UNUSUALLY SEVERE weather of February 1944 prevented both adversaries from undertaking large scale operations. Up in the Abruzzi it snowed incessantly, while on lower ground, on the other hand, there was torrential rain which penetrated low-lying positions. The Garigliano, Liri and Rapido valleys had turned to a swamp, and the front remained quiet, only the artillery keeping up its harassing fire day and night. Under cover of the frequent thick fogs it was possible, however, to carry out local surprise attacks which kept the infantry of both sides on the alert.

The ever-present threat of an outflanking movement by the French Expeditionary Corps (General Juin) was forcing the Germans to bring up reinforcements from the Adriatic front, and to lessen the danger of encirclement, Lt.-General Baade ordered his 90th Panzer Grenadier Division to recapture Monte Castellone in a counter-attack at 4.00 am on 12 February 1944 (Operation 'Michael'). Meanwhile the Americans attacked from Cairo with substantial reserves, using phosphorus hand-grenades for the first time on this sector. These had a devastating effect – the victims burned like torches. The immediate deployment of two battalions of the 7th Indian Brigade (Brigadier Lovett) concentrated near Cairo, also helped to drive back the Germans. The 90th Panzer Grenadier Division was able to hold the summit of Monte Castellone for a mere four hours. The 200th Panzer Grenadier Regiment lost almost 150 men, attacking across ground which afforded no cover, and had to abandon Operation 'Michael'.

On the same day Lt.-General Freyberg took over the Cassino sector with his New Zealand II Corps, formed (as we have seen) from the 2nd New Zealand Division (Brigadier Kippenberger) and the 4th Indian Division (Maj.-General Tuker). Freyberg, who had certainly shown outstanding courage in the First World War, had commanded scarcely more than a division up to now. And the fact that he was directly responsible to the New Zealand government for his soldiers greatly hindered his freedom to make decisions.

The original intention of Lt.-General Clark had been to send in the 4th Indian Division to make the breakthrough to Piedimonte after Monte Cassino had been taken by the US 34th Division (Maj.-General Ryder). Now, after the attack by the Americans had been driven back, Freyberg was to capture Monte Cassino with the 4th Indian Division and build a bridgehead south of Cassino town with the 2nd New Zealand Division. The soldiers of II Corps seemed to possess all the qualities needed to decide the impending battle in their favour: the British and New Zealand troops had repeatedly proved their worth in the fighting in North Africa, while the Gurkhas from Nepal belonged to the most experienced mountain fighters in the British Army, and the Indians were expert at close-quarters fighting.

When the remnants of the battalions of the 34th Division were relieved by the 4th Indian Division, the last fifty Americans to leave their advanced position were almost paralysed with cold and exhaustion, and while they were being carried out of the positions on stretchers some of them fell victim to German artillery fire. The 2nd New Zealand Division took over the sector previously held by the 36th (Texas) Division, but its first planned attack had to be postponed because of continual blizzards.

Freyberg felt that the main reason for the failure of the previous operations by the Americans on the Cassino front was the ability of the Germans to direct their artillery fire from the abbey. The American Generals Keyes and Ryder thought that German fire definitely did not come from the abbey, but from the slopes below. Observation, however, was a different matter. Lt.-General Ira C. Eaker, commanding the Allied Air Force in the Mediterranean, who had himself made a reconnaissance flight, reported that he had seen some radio aerials, and German soldiers running to and fro in the monastery.

Lt.-General Freyberg subsequently asked the commander of the

A mule train travels forward over a snow-clad landscape. The mountainous terrain around Cassino made recourse to such traditional forms of transport a necessity.

A German officer in snow camouflage inspects the far slopes for signs of enemy movement. Against foes such as the French, who could move swiftly and silently by night, such inspections were essential.

US 5th Army for air support for the following day and made the 4th Indian Division's planned attack on Monte Cassino dependent on the previous destruction of the monastery. Lt.-General Clark refused this request in horror, yet there was agreement that it should be left up to Freyberg to decide whether to call on the assistance of the US bomber force, and in the afternoon General Alexander decided that if General Freyberg considered it necessary the abbey was to be bombed. He was sorry that this edifice had to be destroyed but relied on Freyberg's powers of judgement.

The American heavy bombers required for this mission were in Foggia but under the command of General Spaatz's HQ in London. The highest British authorities must therefore have intervened in order to free the bomber units of the 15th Strategic Air Force in Foggia for the air attack on Monte Cassino.

In fact there was not one single German soldier in the abbey at this time. Closest were two tanks of the 15th Panzer Grenadier Division about 300m (330 yards) from the monastery walls, four mortars positioned 400m (440 yards) away, and not far from those an observer post of the 71st Mortar Regiment.

In practice, the plan which Freyberg drew up for the second battle was only an extension of the previous attacks by the US II Corps: Cassino, Monastery Hill and the abbey itself were to be attacked simultaneously from the north and south-east. It meant the continuation of costly frontal attacks on favourably placed and stubbornly defended German positions. These tactics were in complete contrast to the outflanking manoeuvre suggested by General Juin and already partly completed by him. The French general emphasized again that it was useless to gain small tactical successes when there was no carefully thought out strategic plan behind them. Maj.-General Tuker also recommended an indirect advance, similar to General Juin's outflanking movements over the mountains. The suggestions of both generals unfortunately went unheeded.

Meanwhile all the signs pointed to an imminent German counter-attack on the Anzio-Nettuno beach-head. The strength of the 14th Army had been increased to three infantry divisions, one parachute division, two armoured divisions, two Panzer grenadier divisions, four assault gun detachments and several Panther and Tiger tank detachments. The artillery available was almost equal to that of the Allies, excluding their naval artillery. Now Hitler ordered three divisions to attack on a front about 3km (2 miles) wide, and another three divisions to follow on after the breakthrough. The troops were therefore massed in a very confined space and without adequate air defence, at the mercy of the overwhelming air superiority of the Allies. In addition, owing to Hitler's insistence on an immediate start to the operation, the 14th Army was not able to carry out the required preparations with the necessary care.

On Sunday 13 February severe snowstorms raged all day in the Cassino sector.

The 4th Indian Division had received the order to take Monte Belvedere; it turned out, however, that this mountain had already been captured by the French on 26 January. Other, rather less pleasant, news awaited the Sussex Battalion on Point 593, Monte Calvario. According to their plan of the situation it was being held by the Americans; in reality, however, Monte Calvario, including Rocca Janula and the ruins of the medieval castle, had been recaptured by the 3rd Battalion of the 3rd Parachute Regiment on 10 February, and the Americans were just holding out in a small strong-point on the mountain side.

As the whole plan of action for the storming of Monte Cassino by II Corps rested on an attack from the 'safe jumping-off point' of the adjacent Point 593, it became obvious that no-one on the staff of the Corps had bothered to check the precise situation on the sector they had taken over.

On 13 February 1944, also, the Commander-in-Chief of the Polish II Corps, Lt.-General Anders, arrived in Caserta for a meeting with General Alexander. The Polish II Corps numbered about 50,000

An officer of the Polish II Corps interrogates a prisoner from the German army. The relaxed attitudes of both men make it likely that the captive is a Pole conscripted into the Wehrmacht.

soldiers who all had a long and dangerous journey behind them. Many of them had lost their relatives in Nazi concentration camps or in Siberia, and they knew that the end of the war would by no means bring an end to their troubles.

Following the occupation of eastern Poland by Stalin in 1939, 200,000 Polish soldiers were taken prisoner by the Red Army and 1.5 million inhabitants deported to Siberia. There was no change in their fortunes until 22 June 1941, when Hitler attacked the Soviet Union. Churchill now regarded Stalin as his ally in the fight against the Hitler regime, and on 14 August 1941 the Polish government-in-exile signed a treaty with the USSR in London which arranged for independent Polish fighting forces to be formed from prisoners of war and deportees in the Soviet Union. Their commander was to be General Anders, who at that time was still being held in Lublianka, the notorious Moscow prison.

The formation of an army from weakened and destitute men, who often reported barefoot or in rags at the assembly points, was no easy task. It was only with difficulty that these soldiers were provided with the most basic uniform and equipment.

The soldiers spent the winter of 1941/42 in tented camps in the steppes of Central Asia, with temperatures often fifty degrees below freezing. When in the spring of 1942 General Anders still refused to send his convalescent troops to the front, Moscow stopped part of their rations. Only after the intervention of the British and American Governments did Stalin allow the evacuation of some of the soldiers and their families to Iran. By the time the operation ended on 1 September 1942, General Anders had succeeded in evacuating about 40,000 soldiers and officers, with 26,000 women and children. In the Near East he now formed the 5th Kresowa Infantry Division under Maj.-General Sulik. The 3rd Carpathian Rifle Division under Maj.-General Duch was formed from Anders' men and the *Brigada Karpacka* (Brig.-General Kopanski) which had been in Palestine for two years, its soldiers having made their way there from Hungary and Romania and distinguished themselves in the fighting at Tobruk. Similarly, the 2nd Warsaw Armoured Brigade was formed from three motorized lancer regiments under Maj.-General Rakowski. These three formations now made up the Polish II Corps under Lt.-General Anders.

After training for over a year, the 3rd Carpathian Rifle Division embarked at Alexandria on 14 December 1943 and reached Taranto on 21 December. The division was then sent to the Sangro front as part of the British 8th Army. The 5th Kresowa Infantry Division also landed at Taranto in the last week of February 1944. A considerable Polish force was now present in Italy.

Anders wanted to expand his force still further, and on 13 February 1944 he had seen Alexander and Harding, with a new scheme:

> 'The chief subject of the discussions was, once again, the problem of obtaining reinforcements for the Polish II Army Corps. I told him, as I had told General Maitland Wilson, that reinforcements would come over to us from the other side of the front, as all Poles who had been taken by force to serve in the German army would take the first opportunity to escape and join us, or to surrender to the Allies and become prisoners of war. General Alexander agreed that all Polish prisoners of war should be transferred to separate camps, where they would be "screened", so that those found suitable, could be sent to the 7th Reserve Division in the Middle East.'

During the night of 13/14 February a French soldier succeeded in escaping from German captivity and making his way to the Allied lines. He brought with him valuable information about German positions along the mountain ridges north and west of Monastery Hill.

During the night the weather improved and in the early hours of the morning the New Zealand II Corps HQ informed the 4th Indian Division that the bombing of the abbey would take place on the afternoon of 16 February. A few hours later Lt.-General Freyberg drove to the headquarters of the US 5th Army. He wished to inquire personally about the weather forecast. The meteorologist on duty reported to him that rain was to be expected at mid-day on the following day, and so Freyberg decided to bring forward the air attack planned for the afternoon of 16 February to the morning of 15 February, and notified the Air Force accordingly. All staffs were immediately informed of this change. But in the hurry the most important thing was forgotten – communication with the 4th Indian Division. And towards mid-day on 14 February the 1st Royal Sussex Battalion of the 7th Indian Brigade (Brigadier Lovett) took up its positions according to plan on the slopes of Point 593 (Monte Calvario).

On the afternoon of 14 February 1944 some guns of the US 5th Army fired a few dozen shells in the direction of Monastery Hill. They exploded over the abbey and hundreds of leaflets fluttered to the ground. They explained that the monastery was about to be bombarded, and that it should be evacuated.

Meanwhile the paratroopers of *Kampfgruppe* Schulz were still holding out, although almost at the end of their strength, on the slopes above the Via Casilina. Strangely, the Allies had chosen not to take advantage of the opportunity offered by the capture of Monte Belvedere by the French Expeditionary Corps. An advance down to the Via Casilina, over the mountains which towered above Monte Cassino to

Monte Cassino, 17 February 1944: the abbey in ruins following the American bombing raid. Ironically, the destruction of the abbey hindered rather than helped the Allied offensive.

the north, would have allowed Monastery Hill to be captured without firing a single shell on the abbey. Another way of saving Monte Cassino from destruction was by bombing not the abbey, but the precise positions held by *Kampfgruppe* Schulz. In doing this the Allies could have knocked out this section of the Gustav Line and left Monastery Hill alone.

On Tuesday 15 February 1944 at 9.30 am the message arrived at the 7th Brigade's command post that the bombers were already approaching. Brigadier Lovett could do nothing other than accept it. Colonel Glennie, the commander of the Royal Sussex, put it most succinctly: 'They told the monks and they told the enemy but they didn't tell us!'

At 9.45 am 142 B-17 Flying Fortresses from the 15th Strategic Air Force stationed in Foggia (Maj.-General Twining) dropped a total of 253 tons of incendiary and high-explosive bombs. At that moment hundreds of refugees and wounded from the town of Cassino and the surrounding ruined villages were in the chapel for morning service. The second wave, forty-seven twin-engined Mitchells and forty twin-engined Marauders from the Mediterranean Air Force (Lt.-General Eaker) unloaded a further 100 tons of bombs.

For the first time in the history of aerial warfare heavy bombers of strategic air forces were deployed as tactical support for infantry. During the action sixteen heavy bombs inadvertently fell on the headquarters of the US 5th Army in Presenzano, 25km (15 miles) south of Cassino. And the 7th Indian Brigade–itself surprised by the bombing–suffered considerable casualties.

According to the official report of US Air Command, US bombers had dropped 576 tons of bombs on the abbey of Monte Cassino by nightfall, but although the monastery buildings had been destroyed and the outer walls breached, the report admitted that owing to the thickness of the walls the bombs could not demolish everything.

Monastery and basilica were now merely a heap of rubble. Only the strong outer walls of the west wing, the entrance steps and a part of the *torretta* had defied the bombs. Those who ran out of the monastery died under the rain of explosive of the American second wave bombers.

As General Fuller wrote: 'The blame for the failure was debited on the abbey instead of to the hill upon which it stood. . . . Therefore the bombing of the abbey was not so much a piece of vandalism as an act of sheer tactical stupidity.' Indeed, the destruction of the monastery was a considerable disadvantage to the Allies. The abbey, now occupied by the Germans, was transformed into an impregnable fortress with bomb- and artillery-proof subterranean passages and cellars. Churchill: '. . . The Germans had now every excuse for making whatever use they could of the rubble of the ruins, and this gave them even better opportunities for defence than when the building was intact.' Lt.-General Clark: '. . . Not only was the bombing of the abbey an unnecessary psychological mistake in the propaganda field, but it was a tactical military mistake of the first magnitude. It only made the job more difficult, more costly in terms of men, machines and time.'

The Germans now expected a large-scale attack, but nothing of the kind occurred. The 4th Indian Division had no idea that the bombing had been brought forward by a day; it had not prepared an infantry attack and therefore sent out a company of the 7th Brigade to Monte Calvario (Point 593) for detailed reconnaissance. The men did not have enough hand-grenades and mortar ammunition, however, because most of the equipment and ammunition transported by lorries and mules had been lost to enemy artillery fire. The other units of the 4th Division, (a battalion of the 5th Rajputana Rifles and a battalion of 2nd Gurkha Rifles) which were to have taken part in the 7th Brigade's attack on the abbey, were still on the far side of the Rapido.

Thus, wretched co-ordination between ground and air forces had rendered futile the destruction of one of the most significant sites in Christendom, by preventing the 4th Indian Division from being properly prepared for the storming of the abbey after this massive bombing.

On Wednesday 16 February at 6.30 am after an intense preliminary

bombardment, three divisions of the German 14th Army began their attack on both sides of the Aprilia-Anzio road against the Anzio-Nettuno beach-head. Before the action an order of the day from Hitler was read out to the troops in which he demanded the elimination of the Allied beach-head within three days. On account of the Allied naval artillery, however, the German forces could only concentrate in a strictly limited area.

The German attack, supported by 452 guns, was the heaviest of the campaign; a total of 270 tanks, including 75 Tiger tanks, took part. But at once they ran up against stiff Allied resistance; German intentions had been clear because of their troop dispositions.

As the tanks and assault guns stuck fast in the sodden ground, they were forced to advance along the few metalled roads. But then the armoured units could not spread out, and were prey to Allied fighter-bombers and artillery. The infantry was left without support and made only slow progress under severe air attack and a counter-bombardment, which consumed ten times more ammunition than the German. The crack *Infanterie-Lehrregiment* succeeded in penetrating the Allied lines, however, at numerous points along the road to Albano, an area held by the British 1st Division and the US 3rd Division.

At the same time, in the Cassino sector, Allied pursuit bombers were attacking the ruins of the abbey with machine-guns, cannon and fragmentation bombs; but the paratroops sustained no casualties. The

Above: A field dressing station of the US 5th Army at Anzio. The Allied forces prided themselves on ensuring that wounded soldiers received adequate medical attention.

Right: The Abbot of Monte Cassino, Dom Gregorio, is helped into a car by General von Senger und Etterlin during his journey to the Vatican.

Germans now also evacuated the eighty-three year old abbot of the monastery, Don Gregorio Diamare, together with those monks and refugees who had survived the Allied bombing. Some hours later Radio Berlin publicized the text of a declaration signed by the abbot: '. . . I guarantee the truth that no German soldiers were within the walls of the sacred monastery of Cassino at any time . . .'

On the 16th, too, the *Luftwaffe* gained their last success with remote-controlled bombs at Anzio. II *Gruppe** of *Kampfgeschwader* 100 sank the US freighter *Elihu Yale* (7176 gross register tons) and the landing craft LCT-35 which was lying alongside to unload ammunition.

Towards evening on 16 February 1944, thirty-two hours after the bombing of the abbey, one battalion of the 7th Indian Brigade at last crossed the Rapido and advanced in the direction of Monte Cassino. At the foot of the mountain it ran into a mine-field and had to leave some dead and wounded behind. Shortly afterwards the battalion was caught in heavy machine-gun and mortar fire. Twelve officers and 130 men died or were wounded. The rest of the battalion was able to escape and regain the bank of the Rapido.

By Thursday 17 February the German 14th Army had penetrated 4km (2.5 miles) into the Anzio-Nettuno bridgehead. Armoured reserves were now sent in and the attack approached its climax. Low cloud cover that day made effective air support impossible for the Allies, but in spite of heavy artillery support the German troops were only able to make very gradual progress. They did send in 'Goliath', the small remote-controlled exploding tanks, but these met with only limited success.

Six more battalions of the 7th Indian Brigade attempted to storm Monastery Hill, Monte Calvario and Point 404 (situated between the two) on 17 February, but at sunset they were caught in German crossfire. The attack proceeded slowly and with heavy casualties; Allied supporting fire was suppressed because it was feared their own troops might be hit.

The 28th (Maori) Battalion was to carry out an attack across the Rapido with the help of the 4th New Zealand Armoured Brigade. In the evening the Maoris moved into their assembly positions between the Via Casilina and the railway line north-west of Monte Trocchio, and behind them a group from the 4th Armoured Brigade took up position. As darkness fell the Maoris advanced to Cassino station. In spite of fierce fighting they took the station building and pushed on towards the south-west over the Rapido. Having accomplished the river crossing they were ordered to wait for the pursuing tanks, but the armoured vehicles became bogged down on the muddy river bank. The Maori battalion was joined by an engineering battalion, which

Dichiarazione

Don Nicola Clemente Amministratore
della Badia di Montecassino e Don
Francesco Falconio Delegato vescovile
dell'Ufficio Amministrazione della Dioce
di Montecassino, salvatisi dal bombard
mento aereo del giorno 15 febbraio col qu
l'intera Badia veniva distrutta

dichiarano

che nell'interno del Monastero e per
tutto il suo cerchio perimetrale non
esistevano apprestamenti difensivi

The Abbot's declaration that no German soldiers had been stationed in the monastery.

*See note page 53.

A field howitzer of the British 8th Army opens up a night bombardment in support of an Allied assault.

was to clear mines and road-blocks and build bridges over the Rapido. If they could manage that by dawn, about 180 tanks, anti-tank guns and the rest of the division could then follow on.

Towards 11.00 pm the Sussex Battalion was to make a renewed attack on Monte Calvario. The action did not begin until after midnight, however as the mule train with the hand-grenade supplies was delayed, and arrived with only half of the required ammunition. The battalion was plagued by bad luck: when the artillery support opened up, shells fell in the middle of the leading company. As in the previous night, violent machine-gun fire met them after only 50m (165 feet). In the close-quarters combat which developed the advance was repulsed. Now Lt.-General Freyberg split up II Corps. Instead of assaulting the abbey ruins, the Sussex Battalion, reinforced by the Rajputana riflemen, was to attack Monte Calvario.

While shortly after midnight the Maoris stormed the station and

A night artillery bombardment: guns of a battery of the US 5th Army artillery fire on a German position.

took a number of prisoners, the Rajputana moved towards Monte Calvario, through the mountains silhouetted 600m (1970 feet) above the station. Meanwhile both Gurkha battalions pressed on to the abbey about 1000m (1100 yards) away.

At 2.00 am two Gurkha battalions attacked in pale moonlight from the ridge of D'Onofrio (Point 450) in the direction of Monastery Hill. Almost immediately they became caught up in the thorn hedges, laced with mines and barbed wire. In only a few minutes 243 men fell to the machine-gun crossfire and shellfire. One Gurkha battalion succeeded in advancing under cover of darkness to Point 444, about 200m (220 yards) north-west of the abbey, but at dawn they realized that they were hemmed in between the abbey and the German positions on Monte Calvario. In order to avoid further casualties the Gurkhas retreated. The attack by the Sussex Battalion and the Rajputana Rifles on Monte Calvario had to be suspended.

The Maoris who had pressed on to the station also found themselves in a desperate situation, as without effective anti-tank weapons they were endangered by a German counter-attack at any time, and at daybreak they would be clearly visible from the German observation posts on Monastery Hill, the south-east corner of which was only 500m (550 yards) away.

The Allied command now decided to lay a smokescreen around the entire station area as soon as it became light. By dawn on 18 February the engineers had almost finished their work at the station, and behind the advancing Maoris had managed to build a stretch of road almost 2km ($1\frac{1}{4}$ miles) long, along which tanks could be brought forward. By sunrise the Maoris had dug themselves in and secured their new position; they now had to wait for twelve hours, until darkness fell again, to continue their attack. While the battalions of the 4th Indian Division retreated to their initial positions with their wounded, the area around the station in which the Maoris had entrenched themselves still lay under a thick smokescreen.

Towards 3.00 pm German infantry suddenly appeared with two tanks and, skilfully taking advantage of the smokescreen themselves, attacked the station. After a short bitter struggle the Maoris had to retreat, as they lacked armour-piercing weapons. They crossed the Rapido in full flight, leaving dead and wounded behind. The German Panzer grenadiers pursued them almost to Monte Trocchio and only drew back at the approach of darkness.

This Friday also saw von Mackensen's last attempt to force a breakthrough into the Anzio-Nettuno beach-head, using the two divisions still available in reserve. He succeeded in gaining a few more kilometres of ground, but the Allied resistance stiffened more and more. This was probably the bloodiest battle so far between the Germans and the Americans.

In spite of heavy casualties the German units forced back Allied troops, and a fresh attack, reinforced by the 26th Armoured Division (Lt.-General Baron von Lüttwitz), gained further ground in the direction of the coast. However, the US 45th Division and the British 1st and 56th Divisions fought doggedly for the last defensive positions of the bridgehead. Finally, at the Carroceto Marsh, the German advance was halted.

On Saturday 19 February the US 1st Armoured Division and the 3rd Infantry Division penetrated the flank of the German attacking wedge near Anzio. Although they had already approached to within 12km (7 miles) of the coast of the Tyrrhenian Sea, German casualties were so high that Kesselring decided to break off the attack.

At 14.30 hours Maj.-General Westphal, Kesselring's Chief-of-Staff, reported to German High Command that Allied air superiority, obstinate resistance and naval artillery made it impossible to force them back into the sea. He did not know that the Allies, having thrown in their last reserves, were at the same time considering whether to re-embark their forces and abandon the beach-head. Churchill himself realized the dangers of a small advance of the German artillery positions. The issue was one of life and death for the troops of Anzio.

In the morning of 19 February, Lt.-General Anders was informed that the deployment of the Polish II Corps would depend for the time being on developments in the Cassino sector, and the eventual decision would be taken in about three weeks.

After all attempts to capture Monte Cassino had failed, General Alexander that day called off the battle. In the mountains the winter tightened its grip with blizzards and fog; in the valleys it poured with rain, and no aeroplane was to be seen in the overcast sky. Only the Allied artillery kept up its tireless harassing fire.

Allied intentions for the second battle of Cassino had been to relieve the beach-head at Anzio-Nettuno, which was near to collapse. But the inadequate supply of ammunition to units fighting in the mountains, the bad weather which made effective air and heavy weapon support almost impossible, and, above all, the resolute defence, all combined to turn the second battle of Cassino into a German defensive victory and another Allied defeat.

A carrier pigeon is released by a soldier in a British commando observation post. The mountainous terrain hindered radio communication to such an extent that pigeons were frequently used as a substitute. On the right of the picture is a German MP40 submachine-gun.

THIRD PHASE

20 February – 25 March

The Struggle for the Town

Opposite: Men of the 4th Indian Division drag supplies up precipitous, rocky slopes, where they were to fight an exhausting, desperate battle against the German troops.

Bitter Fighting in Cassino

Sunday 20 February 1944
Allied Headquarters announces: On the Fifth Army front at Anzio, our positions have been improved. During the previous 24 hours continuous and violent fighting has taken place with both sides employing tanks, infantry, and strong artillery support. Both sides have also been very active in the air. Heavy casualties have been inflicted on the enemy.

On the main Fifth Army front strong pressure has been maintained against the enemy in Cassino and the mountains west of the town. Newly won hill positions have been consolidated. Elsewhere on this front British troops repulsed two counter-attacks by the enemy. More than 100 prisoners were captured, including three company commanders.

Successful Fighting at Nettuno

Tuesday 22 February 1944
German Supreme Command announces: . . . In Italy our troops were able to improve their positions in several sectors of the Nettuno beach-head, in spite of stubborn resistance by the enemy. Counter-attacks by the enemy against our new lines were repulsed. South of Aprilia enemy forces have been encircled and groups of them are being captured. By day and night German bombers and fighter-bombers continued their attacks on the Nettuno beach-head. In Anzio harbour two merchant ships totalling 9000 gross register tons were seriously damaged by bombs, and several fuel and ammunition dumps destroyed . . .

Free French leaders examine Juin's plans: from left, General de Gaulle, Maj-General de Goislard de Monsabert, the civilian Diethelm, General Juin, and General de Lattre de Tassigny.

All Enemy Attacks Repulsed

Wednesday 23 February 1944
German Supreme Command announces: . . . In Italy the enemy made some unsuccessful localized attacks from the beach-head of Nettuno. During this action an enemy company attacking our positions with armoured support was destroyed. More of the encircled troops south of Aprilia have been taken prisoner. Our fighter-bombers continued to attack vessels unloading in Anzio harbour, causing fresh destruction and serious fires.

Further Successes by Long-Range Artillery

Friday 3 March 1944
German Supreme Command announces: . . . Our troops carried out highly successful raids into the Nettuno beach-head and long-range artillery hit two destroyers and a transport ship, totalling 7000 gross register tons, at Anzio and Nettuno. In a raid on the Adriatic coast three enemy tanks were destroyed and an ammunition and fuel dump blown up, together with its guards.

De Gaulle in Italy

Monday 6 March 1944
The Times *reports:* Algiers wireless announced last night that General de Gaulle has been in Naples, whence he visited the zone of operations and the newly gained positions. He met Generals Alexander, Clark, and Anders.

Polish Corps with 8th Army

Tuesday 7 March 1944
The Times *reports:* The II Polish Corps under General Wladyslaw Anders is fighting in Italy as part of the British Eighth Army. Lieutenant-General Sir Oliver Leese, the successor to General Montgomery, has sent to the Polish Corps a message of welcome, in which he says: 'The fighting quality of the Poles is well known to every British soldier. On my recent visit to the Polish Corps I was struck by the efficiency and keenness of the officers and men. Already, as I could see, these fine troops have begun to learn the technique of battle in this mountainous land. The Polish Corps include men whose fighting qualities were shown as far back as 1940-42 at Tobruck and Gazala. They must be among the oldest members of the Eighth Army.'

Typical German propaganda, dwelling on the Allied failure to break out of the Anzio beach-head, and the casualties the troops were suffering. Apt though this comment might be, the Germans too suffered very heavily in the cramped, static fighting, mainly because of Allied superiority in artillery (including naval artillery) and air power.

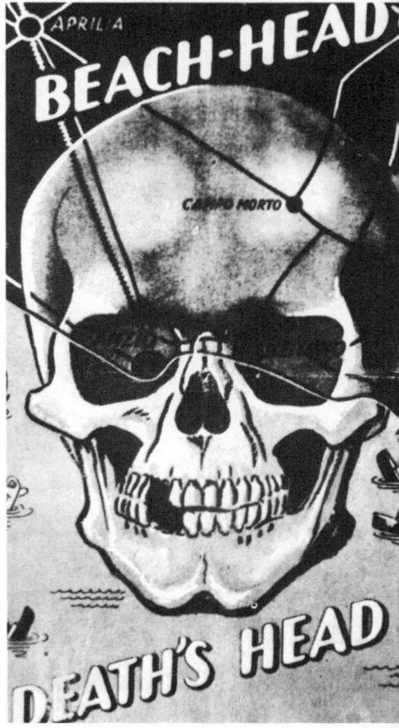

Just Like the Eastern Front

Wednesday 8 March 1944
The German News Bureau reports: During the last four days it has rained incessantly on the Nettuno front. The narrow roads between the mountains and vineyards are turning into a yellow bog, in which only horses and light tractors can make any progress. The marsh, which was drained only a few years ago, seems to want to regain its old mastery. The shell-holes suck up water; the floors of the deep wine cellars fill with mud. The further one penetrates into the deeply echeloned positions the more one has the impression of being on the Eastern Front. The only consolation is the knowledge that the enemy, dug-in even closer to the sea, is doubtless suffering even more from the rain and the rising water table. Just like us, the Allies too have made use of the ravines carved deep into the watercourses to construct their positions. We are living next door to each other, or rather fox-hole to fox-hole. At night the yellow broth pours into the narrow holes which the infantrymen have dug in the steep slopes of the fortified vineyards. Scarcely 150m (160 yards) away it will be exactly the same for the enemy.

Evenly matched adversaries are struggling for supremacy on this battlefield. Yard by yard, the ground must be wrested from the foe; for

German paratroopers watch the bombardment of the town of Cassino on 15 March. The strain of the fighting is showing clearly, but in spite of the enormous weight of explosive used against them, the paratroopers were still able to sustain a dogged close-quarters fight.

every hill and every stream is the nucleus of secure defence. The Anglo-Americans fear nothing so much as a new Dunkirk. The German soldier is acutely aware of this, and therefore the smallest success, if only the gain of one hill or 500 metres (535 yards) of road, may be counted a victory against this stubborn, desperate defence.

Thawing Snow Swells the Rapido

Wednesday 8 March 1944
The Times *reports:* On the main Fifth Army front there were sharp patrol clashes in Cassino, where we hold about one-third of the town. The Germans supported their patrols with intense mortar and machine-gun fire and with grenades. British patrols, clashing with the enemy in the lower Garigliano sector, captured some prisoners. The River Rapido, which flows from the north through Cassino, has risen 3ft. in the past three days with thawing snow from the mountains adding to the prolonged rains.

All Quiet on the Italian Front

Thursday 9 March 1944
German Supreme Command announces: On the Italian fronts patrols and raiding-parties are reported on both sides . . .

Enemy Attacks at Nettuno Collapse

Wednesday 15 March 1944
German Supreme Command announces: . . . After an intense preliminary bombardment from the Nettuno beach-head the enemy made several attacks with tank support; these collapsed with heavy enemy losses, and numerous prisoners were taken. Long-range artillery bombarded enemy shipping off Anzio and Nettuno, hitting a transport and forcing several ships to turn away. North American bombers made another terror raid on Rome. Several parts of the city sustained heavy damage and civilian casualties were high. . . .

Our Paratroops Repulse All Attacks

Thursday 16 March 1944
German Supreme Command announces: . . . After unusually severe bombing on the southern front, the enemy attacked the town of Cassino supported by heavy artillery and tanks. The attacks collapsed in the face of heroic resistance by the 3rd Parachute Regiment commanded by Colonel Heilmann, with valuable support from the 71st Mortar Regiment commanded by Lt.-Colonel Andrae . . .

Another Futile Assault on Cassino

Friday 17 March 1944
German Supreme Command announces: In Italy, after heavy bombing, the enemy made another attack on Cassino using New Zealand, Indian and French troops, with massive artillery and armoured support. An enemy unit which penetrated into the town was immediately thrust back by our brave paratroops. Heavy fighting is still going on. On the other front there was no fighting of any significance . . .

New Zealanders Spearhead Assault

Saturday 18 March 1944
The Times *reports:* The battle for Cassino pursues its grim course across the ruins and rubble of the town. Forces of the Fifth Army have gained all but the south-west part of Cassino, and the Germans are making a determined effort to retain what hold they still have in that part of town. New Zealand troops formed the spearhead of the assault on Cassino, and, with Indian troops, have also taken hill positions over-looking the town. Remnants of buildings and masses of debris have been transformed by the enemy into strong-points, each one of which has become a sniper's post.

German troops waiting with a self-propelled gun (a Sturmgeschütz *III) in a ruined house, just before the Allied attack. They have set up racks of grenades, instantly ready for use. In the house-to-house fighting, grenades were used in vast quantities.*

Grim Struggle for the Centre of Cassino

Saturday 18 March 1944
German Supreme Command announces: In the Nettuno beach-head only local fighting is reported. But on the southern front the grim struggle for the centre of Cassino continues with undiminished violence. Cassino station was lost after a hard fight. In the ruins of the town bitter fighting is still going on . . .

Vigorous German Counter-attack in Cassino

Sunday 19 March 1944
German Supreme Command announces: Our own assault troops destroyed numerous pockets of resistance in the Nettuno beach-head. The enemy suffered heavy and bloody casualties. Prisoners were taken. At Cassino the enemy continued his strong attacks with tank support. In severe fighting, and with effective support from our ground attack aircraft they were beaten back. In a vigorous counter-attack the ruined castle to the north-west of the town was recaptured. On the remaining front the day was uneventful . . .

A shell explodes as smoke drifts across the battered town. Smokescreens were used to protect the Allied forces in the town of Cassino itself; but they also allowed the Germans to regroup in safety.

Germans Still Hold Out

Monday 20 March 1944
The Times *reports:* Little by little the enemy is being blasted out of his positions at Cassino. By last evening the New Zealanders, fighting their way through the rubble of demolished houses, had quenched German resistance in the town except for two strong-points, consisting of about half a dozen houses each, on the western edge. On the previous night, supported by tanks, they had completed the conquest of the railway station. Early yesterday morning the enemy made an attempt to regain a footing in the station, but the attacking party were smashed, and some prisoners were taken.

Meanwhile our positions gained in the previous two days fighting by Indian troops on the slopes below the abbey were consolidated and extended. Point 165, alias Castle Hill, which is a low spur jutting out above the town, and which had been captured and then lost, was recaptured and held against a counter-attack.

The New Zealanders' progress across the wreck of the town has not been easy. The Germans had prepared deep shelters in the hillside caves, whence they emerged after the bombardment and resisted stubbornly. The movement of our supporting tanks was made difficult by the immense mounds of rubble caused by our bombing.

The grim view across the town after the bombing, showing the difficulties facing the attackers: mines, barbed wire, and heaps of rubble, concealing enemy positions.

In Cassino All Enemy Attacks Meet a Bloody End in German Fire

Tuesday 21 March 1944
German Supreme Command announces: From the Nettuno beach-head only frequent reconnaissance activity is reported. In the town of Cassino yesterday all enemy attacks again came to a bloody halt under the fire of the brave defenders. North-west of the town an enemy unit was surrounded. Enemy losses amount to many times our own.

In the Crater Fields of Cassino

Tuesday 21 March 1944
Völkischer Beobachter *reports:* Last Wednesday morning, in beautiful sunshine following a relatively quiet night punctuated by the usual raids, hundreds of four-engined bombers, pursuit bombers and escorts hurled themselves upon the Cassino area in deeply echeloned waves for almost three hours, and it was plain that after barely two weeks of calm on the Cassino front the fourth large-scale attack was about to begin. An Indian division attacked from north of the town and a New Zealand division made another frontal assault against the bulwark which till then had put up such a glorious and extraordinarily

Right: German paratroops, wearing the regulation loose smocks and their distinctive cut-down helmets with their winged emblem. The esprit de corps *of this parachute division, carried it through the grim test of Cassino.*

Below: German propaganda, but an all too accurate impression of the futile Allied offensives in the mountains.

powerful defence. The screaming bombs, some of which were dropped from a very low altitude, seemed to engulf the whole area; and they were followed by choking clouds of grey-white dust from the exploding houses and freshly raked ruins. Many centres of resistance were buried by the collapsing walls, and some heavy weapons were temporarily eliminated because the surging hail of debris and rubble was falling too thickly on the defenders and their weapons . . . But even now, in spite of the heaviest air and ground bombardment of our positions so far, the enemy had deluded himself . . . Bitter resistance, above all by the paratroops who again defied death in their defence of this position on the southern front, meant that the first day brought the adversary only minimal territorial gains in a totally ruined town, and, as in all his attacks, he again had to suffer the severest losses . . .

Slow but Steady Progress

Wednesday 22 March 1944

Allied Headquarters announces: Very heavy hand-to-hand fighting continues in Cassino and on the hills above the town. Our troops are making slow but steady progress against strong opposition. On the remainder of the main Fifth Army front and in the Fifth Army allied bridgehead patrols were active. Sharp patrol clashes occured on the Eighth Army front.

Fight for Hangman's Hill

Wednesday 22 March 1944
The Times *reports:* The struggle at Cassino goes on with unabated fury. Down on the edges of the town the New Zealanders are slowly reducing the enemy's strong-points, while on the slopes of Monastery Hill troops are still hanging on gamely to their precarious vantage points. The enemy still holds Point 165 alongside Castle Hill, but Castle Hill itself has been defended successfully by the allies against repeated counter-attacks and Point 435, commonly known as Hangman's Hill, which is the highest outpost yet gained in the assault on the abbey from below, remains in our hands.

Twice in three days Invaders have roared over the hill dropping supplies for the garrison at this post, which can hardly be reached by carriers even at night, as the tracks have been damaged by bombs and shells. Hangman's Hill is a plateau of some 250ft. below the abbey. Nobody quite knows how the troops which captured it got there, but they are there.

New Zealanders in the ruins. The shattered buildings were ideal for siting defensive positions, as attacking troops such as these found to their cost time after time.

'They are Offering Fearful Resistance'

Wednesday 22 March 1944
Völkischer Beobachter *reports:* The heroic fight of the German troops in Cassino elicits the highest admiration and respect even from the enemy press. The military correspondents of English newspapers are drawing conclusions which are not exactly flattering to the Anglo-American high command. The London News Service, which would certainly like to offer better news from Cassino, cannot help saying a few words about the exemplary conduct of the German defenders. It explained in a night-time broadcast from Naples on 20 March that these are no ordinary German troops, but specially trained, party members and soldiers of the 1st Parachute Division. They are tough, but no suicide squad. They are offering fearful resistance.

Several Attacks Repulsed

Thursday 23 March 1944
German Supreme Command announces: At Cassino several attacks with tank support to the north of the town were repulsed by our concentrated defensive fire.

German Resistance

Thursday 23 March 1944
Völkischer Beobachter *reports:* The opening phase of the enemy attack

on the ruins of Cassino on 15 March was saturation bombing (by hundreds of aircraft) in a confined space, on a scale probably unique in the course of the war so far. Although this temporarily knocked out some parts of the German defence, our paratroops dug themselves and their weapons out of the rubble-strewn wreckage of their cover-holes, renewed the fight against the advancing enemy from the rear, and fought their way through to the positions of their comrades.

A characteristic example of the fierceness of this battle was provided by one corporal. Hit by several shell splinters and covered with blood, he collapsed unconscious by his machine-gun. The New Zealanders storming forwards took him for dead. When he recovered consciousness shortly afterwards, however, he at once took stock of the new situation. Entirely on his own, he directed his machine-gun fire in a surprise attack on the advancing infantry platoons, who flung themselves to the ground or fled. He himself sprang from shell-hole to shell-hole spraying bursts of machine-gun fire, until he got back to his unit.

During the changing fortunes of the next few days' fighting, paratroops commanded by Lt.-General Heidrich, holder of the *Eichenlaub* [a military decoration], who himself led attack and defence from the midst of his troops, eventually brought the enemy assault to a halt and sealed off the point of entry.

In the course of their own counter-attacks our paratroops succeeded in trapping many enemy troops between the town and the ruined monastery (destroyed by the Anglo-Americans). These troops have, since then, lain under continual German artillery fire. The enemy is supplying its trapped forces from the air and trying to bring up reinforcements; but just as on 20 March, all attempts to break out and all relief efforts have been fruitless.

Resolute German Defence

Friday 24 March 1944

The Times *reports:* It is more than a week now since Cassino was bombed and blasted on a scale unprecedented for a target of comparable size; immediately afterwards it endured artillery bombardment of scarcely less magnitude. Cassino was reduced to rubble. But rubble becomes a ready-made fighting pitch for determined, audacious, resourceful troops; and those were the troops which the Germans had sent to Cassino deliberately to hold the place as long as possible.

Perhaps three companies were wiped out and much equipment lost in the bombing and shelling, but the men who appeared from the rubble were men frantically determined to hold Cassino as long as possible. They appeared from deep cellars that had been left unscathed by bombing and shelling; others dug their way through the debris, and even when cornered refused to surrender. Such are the men of the German 1st Parachute Division. . . . Cassino will inevitably fall, but the longer that fall is delayed the stronger are the Germans making their next defensive positions in the Adolf Hitler Line to the west. The balance of casualties in this grim, prolonged struggle has been definitely in our favour, and some companies of the Germans' 1st Parachute Division have been reduced to a handful of men.

The Anglo-Americans Cease Their Attacks

Friday 24 March 1944

German Supreme Command announces: In Italy yesterday, following his heavy losses, the enemy did not continue his attacks on Cassino. On both fronts there is only local fighting.

German paratroops in the ruins of the monastery with an MG42 machine-gun. Such a position could pin down large numbers of Allied troops before it was spotted and counter fire directed at it; and then the Germans could easily find another such post.

In the ruins of the monastery, a German officer briefs his men before they set out on a reconnaissance mission.

No More Difficult Task than the Capture of Cassino

Friday 24 March 1944

Völkischer Beobachter *reports:* In a commentary on the situation the British broadcaster W. N. Young gave his views on the heavy fighting in Italy. In this war so far, he considered there had been no more difficult task than the capture of Cassino. In respect of the fighting there, a certain disappointment was becoming evident in English circles, since the air experts had been a little over-optimistic about the effects of their massed attacks. General Eaker had been so enthusiastic about his own achievement that he had unfortunately overestimated it. The outstanding German soldiers concentrated here could only be countered by the best troops.

The cold February was drawing to an end; in the Campagna it was still damp, but on the coast orange blossom heralded the spring.

During the night of 19/20 February 1944 the 1st Battalion of the 211th Grenadier Regiment undertook a reconnaissance across the Rapido in the direction of Monte Trocchio; but the heavily armed platoon of sixty men was taken prisoner without firing a shot. They had, too, been equipped with the new MP 44 assault rifles which should not have been allowed to fall into enemy hands.

Lt.-General Heidrich (the photograph was taken when he was a colonel) wearing his Knight's Cross. As commander of the 1st Parachute Division, Heidrich was to contain the Allied attacks after the bombing of the town.

On Sunday 20 February the 1st Parachute Division (Lt.-General Heidrich) began to relieve the 90th Panzer Grenadier Division (Lt.-General Baade), which had played such a decisive part in previous defensive successes. The 1st Battalion of the 3rd Parachute Regiment under Major Böhmler took over the position on Monte Cassino, while the 2nd Battalion (Captain Foltin) took over the positions in the town. To their right was the 15th Panzer Grenadier Division (Maj.-General Rodt), on the left flank the 5th Mountain Division (Colonel Schrank) with the 44th Infantry Division (Lt.-General Franek). The relief was carried out in a pouring rain, which turned the paths and mountain tracks into rivers of mud. The dug-outs were often under water and first had to be baled out with steel helmets. By day, movement was scarcely possible in the dug-outs, never mind outside.

The 1st Parachute Division had been in action without a break since the Allied landing on 9 September and had been considerably reduced in strength. Now it had to cover a sector 13km (9 miles) wide which extended from Cassino station to Monte Cairo, almost 1700m (5600 feet) high. Cassino town was defended by the 2nd Battalion (Captain Foltin) of the 3rd Parachute Regiment, reinforced by the 10th Company and an assault gun battery for anti-tank defence. The 1st Battalion of the 3rd Parachute Regiment took up position on Monastery Hill and the surrounding heights were held by the 1st and 4th Parachute Regiments.

On Monday 21 February 1944 the preparations for Operation 'Dickens', a fresh attack in the Cassino sector planned by Lt.-General Freyberg, were complete. It was to begin on 24 February 1944 provided that the ground was firm enough for tanks. The New Zealand II Corps would take part, with two infantry divisions and a tank regiment.

As before, it was decided to make a frontal assault on Cassino and Monastery Hill rather than to approach them from the flank. Massed air forces and artillery, of a magnitude rare in the history of war, were to pave the way for the assault troops. The difference between Operation 'Dickens' and the previous battle was that the breakthrough would take place at only one point, about 1.5km (1 mile) wide, with an enormous input of material.

Allied transport laboriously moves up along the snowy roads.

On Tuesday 22 February, after the German counter-attack on the Anzio-Nettuno beach-head had already been driven back, Maj.-General Lucas was relieved of his command. The US VI Corps was now taken over by Maj.-General Truscott, formerly commander of the US 3rd Division.

On Wednesday 23 February, the weather worsened. It poured with rain for the whole day, and Operation 'Dickens' had to be postponed; but no-one guessed that it would rain incessantly for almost three weeks.

Meanwhile the 1st Battalion of the 3rd Parachute Regiment had turned the ruins of the abbey into a fortress. Four heavy and two light machine-guns, in addition to two medium mortars, protected Monastery Hill. Several artillery observers and eighty paratroopers occupied the shell-proof subterranean passages.

On Thursday 24 February winter returned to the Abruzzi with the utmost severity. The mountains lay under a thick blanket of snow. Icy storms paralyzed all movement on the front. Only the artillery carried on its fire and counter-fire.

On Friday 25 February General Wilson was ordered to give the campaign in Italy absolute priority over all other operations in the Mediterranean area.

Not until Monday 28 February did Field-Marshal Kesselring order three German divisions to renew attacks on the Anzio-Nettuno beach-head. Owing to the persistent rain, however, the German tanks stuck fast in the mud and the infantrymen sank in up to the knees. The weather prevented the Allied air forces from going into action, and for that reason US artillery fire was all the more intense.

On Tuesday 29 February, LXXVI Panzer Corps (Panzer General Herr) was also thrown into the fighting at Nettuno. But the weather had improved meanwhile, and so Allied naval artillery and aircraft could be deployed; their support enabled the US 3rd Division to stand firm against the German attack.

On the afternoon of 1 March Kesselring called off the German attack. The attempt to eliminate the Allied beach-head without adequate air support had at last failed, and the 14th Army (Colonel-General von Mackensen) went on the defensive, constructing a set of defences in depth to hold up the expected Allied offensive in the direction of Rome.

On Thursday 2 March the 2nd New Zealand Division was dealt a severe blow – its commander, Brigadier Kippenberger, was badly wounded. He had been making an inspection of the batteries on Monte Trocchio when he stepped on one of the notorious German wooden mines, on a path supposedly clear, and lost both feet. Command was taken over by Maj.-General Parkinson.

A sniper of the Grenadier Guards takes careful aim from his concealed lair. As in all street fighting of the Second World War, notably at Stalingrad, sniping came into its own in ruined houses.

At this time the Western Supreme Commanders were under severe political pressure. On the Eastern Front the Red Army had already captured large parts of Eastern Poland and reached Romania. Stalin made repeated complaints to his allies that he was having to bear the main burden of the fight against Hitler unaided, because the Western Allies were merely conducting limited land warfare. In order to counter this criticism, the latter felt constrained to make a renewed attack at Cassino, even without appropriate preparation.

On Friday 10 March, the troops of the New Zealand II Corps, who were to attack in the Cassino sector, at last received a plan of the town on which the German machine-gun positions, mine-fields and anti-tank weapons were marked. It was clear that the town could only be reached by a narrow road; the extensive mine-fields could only be threaded through in single file. Even the 5th Indian Brigade, which was to attack Monte Cassino itself, had to negotiate the same stretch

Lt.-General Leese (centre, standing) and his staff watch the progress of Allied operations in the town from the headquarters of the New Zealand Corps at Cervaro.

until shortly before they reached Monastery Hill. Thus, in this battle too, Lt.-General Freyberg stuck to his plan for an extremely risky frontal attack by the separated units. On Saturday 11 March the so-called 'Cavendish Road' in the Cassino sector was completed. This tank road about 4m (13 feet) wide – built by the New Zealand engineers in eleven days – ran from Cairo over Massa Albaneta and now afforded access to Monastery Hill from the rear. As the route could be seen from German observation posts, screens first had to be set up which hid the work columns as well as the completed sections of road.

It had been raining in the Liri valley for almost three weeks, and the troops increasingly suffered from nervous tension caused by the daily postponement of the attack. In spite of the relative quiet the situation of the Germans was no better, as most were lying in open country. The men were worn down by holding out for days on end in their constricted cover on bare rock – a groundsheet the only protection against the weather – as well as by the lack of all but the most primitive sanitary arrangements. Snow and rain soaked through their clothing, and rations consisted of tinned food warmed up on spirit stoves.

On Sunday 12 March 1944 the weather improved, and the Allied meteorologists were of the opinion that by 15 March conditions would at last be more favourable for Operation 'Dickens'. During the evening of 14 March Lt.-General Freyberg pulled back his troops some way from Cassino, so that they would not be endangered by the planned bombing of the town. This precaution was concealed from the Germans.

In the early morning of 15 March all the top brass, including the Commander-in-Chief of the Allied Forces, General Alexander, assembled in the headquarters of II Corps in Cervaro, barely 5km (3 miles) from Cassino. The brilliant blue sky promised a beautiful day and the view towards Cassino was superb. On the second floor of this old farm-house on the slopes of Monte Velletri, these officers waited anxiously for the results of an experiment. For the first time on the Italian front a town was to be obliterated by carpet-bombing. And this promised to be a unique experience for all present. There was relief that the problem which had caused so much concern over the past weeks was at last going to be solved in this way. The Allied commanders were convinced that scarcely anyone would be able to escape from the inferno which would erupt in the valley in a few minutes' time. After all, about five tons of explosive had been provided for every German soldier in Cassino. And the Allied commanders secretly hoped that, whatever else happened, the nerve of the German paratroops would break, as, in their opinion, no-one who survived this bombardment could remain in their right mind.

At 8.30 am formations of four-engined B-17 bombers appeared

according to plan and laid the first carpet of bombs over a sector barely 1500m (1 mile) wide and 500m (530 yards) deep: the third battle of Cassino had begun. At that moment the generals had no idea that the carpet-bombing itself would deprive them of victory in this phase of the battle; for the débris left behind by the bombers would bar the way for their own tanks.

A British war correspondent noted: 'I remember no spectacle in war so gigantically one-sided. Above, the beautiful, arrogant silver-grey monsters performing their mission with what looked from below like a spirit of utter detachment; below, a silent town, suffering all this in complete passivity.'

The first formation was followed at intervals of 10-15 minutes by further attacking waves. This drama continued for a good four hours.

The aircraft had taken off from airfields in Italy, North Africa and England; there was a total of 575 medium and heavy bombers, besides 200 fighter-bombers. General Eaker, Commander of the Mediterranean Allied Air Force (MAAF), had concentrated the strongest air forces which had ever been assembled in the Mediterranean theatre of

The bombing of the town – an act of destruction which failed to give the Allies the victory they were struggling for. In the conditions of the Cassino battle, mere weight of explosive was not sufficient to guarantee success.

A British unit moves up to the front carrying a Vickers heavy machine-gun along the narrow mountain paths.

At 3.30 pm, after this mighty preliminary bombardment, the combined infantry and tanks attacked what remained of Cassino. About 400 tanks, followed by New Zealand and Indian infantry, advanced into the ruins from the north and towards Rocca Janula (Point 193). They hardly expected any further German resistance, and the tank commanders were standing in open turrets . . .

About 100 German soldiers had survived the bombing, and when the New Zealand 6th Infantry Brigade approached the first heaps of rubble they were surprised by intense defensive fire. A bitter struggle now took place among the ruined houses. The mountains of débris and enormous bomb craters blocked the path of the tanks, and although engineers and tank crews now worked together to clear lanes through which the tanks could advance, the Allies suffered severe casualties in making the slightest progress because it became absolutely impossible for the tanks of the New Zealand 4th Armoured Brigade to support the infantry.

By nightfall the New Zealand 25th Battalion had penetrated about 200m (220 yards) into the centre of the town. Rocca Janula, which surveyed the whole town, was taken only after a hard fight.

The German strong-point in the ruins of the Continental Hotel, defended by the men under *Stoßtruppführer Oberfeldwebel* Neuhoff (from the 2nd Battalion of the 3rd Parachute Regiment), prevented the New Zealand 24th and 26th Battalions from reaching the Via Casilina. The only German assault gun still intact, which stood in the hotel's entrance hall, drove back the tank attacks.

On this first day of the assault, Lt.-General Freyberg made a crucial error. Apart from one single company, no infantry reinforcements were ordered forward when the tanks stuck in the rubble.

In the evening, about two-thirds of Cassino was occupied by the New Zealanders, but the Germans were holding the town centre as well as the station, thereby making it impossible to cross the town and attack the Via Casilina.

After sunset heavy rain set in again, and the débris became a muddy porridge. Under cover of darkness and rain Lt.-General Heidrich was able to filter reinforcements into Cassino. In any case, the New Zealand attack, which was carried out in the most confined area, was too weak, too hesitant and too limited to prevent the Germans from sending in further reinforcements.

The pressure on the town's defenders was relieved by fire from German artillery and rocket-launchers positioned on the surrounding hills, which harassed the troop dispositions outside Cassino and the New Zealand attack itself.

On this first day, from 12.30 am to 8.00 pm, the Allied artillery had fired a total of 195,969 shells, 1200 tons altogether or the equivalent of

Allied troops in the ruins of the church at Sant' Angelo during a break in the action. The man nearest the camera is examining a German MG42 machine-gun.

275 lorry-loads, onto the town and Monastery Hill. General Alexander telegraphed Churchill that he doubted whether any other troops than the paratroops could have stood up to such an ordeal and then gone on fighting with such ferocity.

Now Lt.-General Freyberg ordered an attack on Monastery Hill. Towards midnight the Rajputana Rifles from the Essex Battalion of the 5th Indian Brigade succeeded in advancing to Rocca Janula (Point 193), relieving the New Zealanders there and reaching Point 165.

Rocca Janula – known also as Castle Hill, as there was the ruin of an ancient Roman citadel on the summit – was one of the most important sectors on the approaches to the abbey, since it was joined to Monastery Hill by a saddle of rock. And the Germans knew only too well that the fate of the abbey would depend on the fight for Point 193.

Of the 2nd Company of the 3rd Parachute Regiment, who had been defending this sector, only a corporal was still alive. After the

Shortly before sunrise on 17 March shock troops from the 1st Battalion of the 3rd Parachute Regiment moved out of the monastery ruins to take Hangman's Hill. In an immediate counter-attack the Gurkhas forced the Germans to retreat. In the town itself during the day, a short truce was agreed so that both sides could recover their dead and wounded. The medical orderlies assisted each other and the New Zealanders even handed over some stretchers to the Germans.

In the early hours of the morning of Saturday 18 March, the Motorcycle Company of the 1st Parachute Division waded through the icy Rapido with the intention of recapturing the station. Shortly before, the men had been caught by their own rocket fire and suffered heavy casualties. At 3.40 am they reached the engine-shed which was guarded by the New Zealanders. Firing from some tanks and from machine-gun nests fortified by sandbags halted the German attack.

A medical team treats a wounded soldier in the rubble of the town. They had to give what treatment they could before the severely wounded were carried back by stretcher.

At 3.50 pm forty-eight twin-engined US bombers dropped a number of containers on Hangman's Hill in order to supply the Gurkhas cut off there. Most of them fell into no-man's land, German hands, or rolled into the gorges, but with the scant ammunition and weapons which reached them, the Gurkhas were to make a renewed attack on the monastery the next morning. Two companies of the Essex Battalion were ordered to advance from the fort on Rocca Janula and reinforce them. The remainder of the garrison was ordered to mop up the area around Rocca Janula and occupy Point 263.

After most of the town and the station had been captured, Allied engineers worked feverishly to construct the necessary bridges and to clear the streets. To shield them from the gaze of German artillery observers, the engineers worked under a smoke screen. But at the same time, the troops in the town had to fortify their positions, as the smoke afforded the Germans welcome cover for an attack. A German soldier fighting in the ruins wrote:

> 'Suddenly there was a loud whistling and whirring above us. We stared at each other, there was another loud "ping" and the sound of stone being hit. Hissing, heavy greyish-blue smoke poured out of the pot-shaped contents of these shells . . . In a flash we went over everything we had heard about gas attacks. Meanwhile the insidious grey haze had enveloped us. The crackling in the air went on. The nearest hills appeared as shadows through the grey veil. Eventually we decided the stinking stuff was a smokescreen, and made a virtue out of necessity. For the first time in almost two months we could walk upright by day in this terrain, avoiding of course the disgusting smoke-pots.'

On Sunday 19 March at 4.00 am, the Motorcycle Company of the 1st Parachute Division retreated across the Rapido after twenty-four hours of fighting. They had been reduced to nineteen men; numerous dead and over fifty badly wounded men had to be left behind.

British soldiers in the valley of the Gari. They have just captured a German machine-gun nest, which appears to have been vacated in a hurry: the machine-gun (with belt of amunition in position) has been left behind, and so has a helmet.

At dawn the Maoris began their attack on the Continental Hotel, in order to push through to the Via Casilina, while at the same time the New Zealand 25th Battalion stormed towards the strong points held by the German paratroopers in the north-west of Cassino. Bitter close combat developed again and again amid the mountains of rubble, but the Germans were able to contain both attacks by mid-day.

At 5.30 am both battalions of the Essex Regiment had already left the fort on Rocca Janula and were clambering up Hangman's Hill in order to reinforce the Gurkhas, as planned, in their attack on Monastery Hill. The 1st Battalion of the 4th Parachute Regiment attacked simultaneously in the direction of Rocca Janula. They reached the walls of the fort where a completely bewildered group of about 150 men hastily improvised a defence, driving off those paratroopers who climbed the medieval walls with rifle-butts or knives. The 5th Indian Brigade repulsed the German attack close to Rocca Janula, and both the English battalions went on clambering up Hangman's Hill while watching this battle from above.

At 8.00 am the 1st Battalion of the 4th Parachute Regiment again attacked Point 193 without success. And just as both the Essex Regiment battalions were at last reaching the summit of Hangman's Hill the third German attack on the fort was being repulsed with heavy German casualties. After that the British commanding officer on Rocca Janula, Major Beckett, agreed to a two-hour truce to recover the

Kesselring visits the front. His defensive strategy depended upon the paratroops hanging on grimly at Cassino, for if the Allies broke through to the Liri valley, the road to Rome would be open, and the entire German position in Italy in jeopardy.

On 24 March 1944, however, only one day after the battle for Cassino had been broken off, preparations began for the next offensive. In order to avoid a further disappointment, it was decided to destroy the supply lines and communications of Army Group C (Field-Marshal Kesselring). From this day on, 360 machines of the Mediterranean Allied Air Force (Lt.-General Eaker) were deployed round the clock in Operation 'Strangle'. Every railway line, every road, the air-bases, the harbours, all passes joining Italy with Austria and Germany, even individual soldiers were the targets, especially of the fighter-bombers. Road and rail traffic was brought to a complete standstill by day. The lorries and transport columns only dared to travel at night or in bad weather.

The fighting may have been broken off in the Liri valley for forty-eight hours, but the Gurkha Battalion was still hanging on to its positions on Hangman's Hill. The previous weekend they had been reinforced by some Rajputana Rifles bringing supplies, and on Sunday morning men of the Essex Regiment had joined them to take part in the attack on the abbey which had then been called off. For eight days and nights they all held out on a bare slope 200m (220 yards) across. As they were lying close to the abbey, and the only cover was the summit of the mountain itself, half of them had to be ready for action day and night. In the afternoon of 24 March the wounded descended the mountain in small groups, under the protection of the Red Cross flag, to Rocca Janula. The 1st Battalion of the 4th Parachute Regiment let them pass without firing a shot.

At 10.15 am the weary Gurkhas began the retreat proper from Hangman's Hill. Eight officers and 117 soldiers of the 400 who had stormed Hangman's Hill a week before crept down the mountain covered by artillery fire. They slipped unmolested through the 200m (220 yard) wide gap between the fort and Cassino, and reached the ruins of the town shortly before midnight.

The third battle of Cassino was designed to relieve the Anzio-Nettuno beach-head, but the indecision of Lt.-General Freyberg had contributed to its failure. At each critical moment he had hesitated to commit his reserves and had frittered away his resources piecemeal. In so doing, Freyberg achieved exactly what he had hoped to avoid – a protracted loss of life at Cassino. In the words of Lt.-General von Senger, '. . . This battle will probably go down in history as one of the most incomprehensible plans of the war.'

Thus the third battle of Cassino also ended in a clear victory for the German defence. The entrance to the Liri valley remained closed, the road to Rome was still barred. German casualties, however, were high; most had been sustained in the air attack on 15 March 1944, and the subsequent concentrated artillery bombardment. A total of 588,649 shells had been fired by the Allies during the eight-day battle.

As was the case in the second battle of Cassino, a frontal attack on Monastery Hill had been doomed to failure from the beginning, because there had been no serious attempt to pin down reserves by threatening the German flanks at the same time.

The decisive significance of events between 15 and 23 March lay elsewhere. For the third battle of Cassino was a turning-point in the conduct of Allied tank warfare. Up to this battle the accepted principle was that a tank attack with air and artillery support could only be repulsed by anti-tank units. The fighting of the German 3rd Parachute Regiment in and on both sides of Cassino showed, however, that well-trained infantry armed with modern weapons, in favourable terrain, was quite capable of successfully standing its ground in a major battle against armoured units.

The stubborn resistance of the Germans at Cassino, which the Allies had been vainly attacking for three months, drew the attention of the world to this theatre of war. For Nazi propaganda Monte Cassino was a welcome opportunity to lull the German people with unfounded optimism about the defensive capabilities of the *Reich*.

Gurkhas of the 4th Indian Division in house-to-house fighting. They were some of the best troops for this sort of warfare, as they relished close combat and still carried the deadly kukri, *a heavy, curved slashing knife. Each soldier here is wearing a* kukri *on the back of his belt.*

Hill within the town; our artillery concentrated their fire on the Continental Hotel. Because of the difficulties of maintaining supplies, hitherto dropped by air, the Gurkhas and New Zealanders who gained positions on the eastern slopes of Monastery Hill on March 15 have now been withdrawn.

Enemy Soldiers Destroyed in the Mountains Near Cassino

Friday 31 March 1944
German Supreme Command announces: . . . In Italy yesterday there was only local fighting. A group of enemy soldiers, hemmed in for some time south-west of Cassino and offering fierce resistance, has been destroyed. The enemy lost numerous dead and many prisoners, military equipment of all kinds and weapons were taken. Our own shock troops took some of the enemy's strong points in a sudden attack on the north of the town. In other successful raids four enemy tanks were destroyed by short-range weapons . . .

Collapse of Enemy Attacks

Saturday 1 April 1944
German Supreme Command announces: In Italy, enemy drives against the east of Cassino collapsed. Shock troops blew up enemy pockets of resistance and command posts and ammunition dumps were set on fire by our artillery.

Secret Report of the SS Security Service on the Internal Political Situation

6 April 1944 (green series)
Reports on the development of public opinion: . . . 4. The progress of the fighting in Italy is the only thing at the moment that gives us reason to hope that 'we can still manage it'. It has demonstrated that we are equal to far superior adversaries. There is a belief that even an invasion from the west could not assume dangerous dimensions. However, the question is often asked whether, on the strength of his experiences in Italy, the enemy might not postpone further or cancel altogether the invasion which we expect and desire . . .

All Quiet in Italy

Monday 10 April 1944
German Supreme Command announces: . . . In Italy the day was uneventful . . .

A paratrooper dashes across a stretch of open ground as smoke billows from a smoke pot. Smoke was one of the main ways of concealing preparations for attack and counter-attack from the enemy.

Another Success by our Aircraft at Nettuno

Wednesday 10 May 1944
German Supreme Command announces: On the Italian southern front several enemy drives were repulsed. Shock troops blew up numerous enemy strongholds. Bombers attacked shipping targets in the Nettuno beach-head with great success. Two freighters totalling 5000 gross register tons, two large landing craft and a destroyer were badly hit. It is probable that some of these ships were put out of action.

Heavy Enemy Losses in the Beach-Head

Thursday 11 May 1944
German Supreme Command announces: In the Nettuno beach-head several enemy attacks collapsed under concentrated defensive fire. In the fighting here over the last few days the 10th Company of the 8th Motorized Brandenburg Grenadier Regiment, led by First Lieutenant Thielmann, have particularly distinguished themselves.

Victory Assured

Friday 12 May 1944
General Alexander to Allied forces: We are going to destroy the German armies in Italy. Fighting will be hard and bitter, and perhaps long, but you are warriors and soldiers of the highest order who for

Paratroops manoeuvre their 7.5 cm anti-tank gun into position in the undergrowth. Both they and the gun are heavy camouflaged. This anti-tank gun, designed to take on the heavily armoured Soviet tanks, was capable of doing great damage to the more lightly armed Sherman – the main battle tank of the western Allies.

more than a year have known only victory. You have courage, determination, and skill. You will be supported by overwhelming air forces, and in guns and tanks we far outnumber the Germans.

No armies have ever entered battle before with a more just and righteous cause. So, with God's help and blessing, we take the field confident of victory.

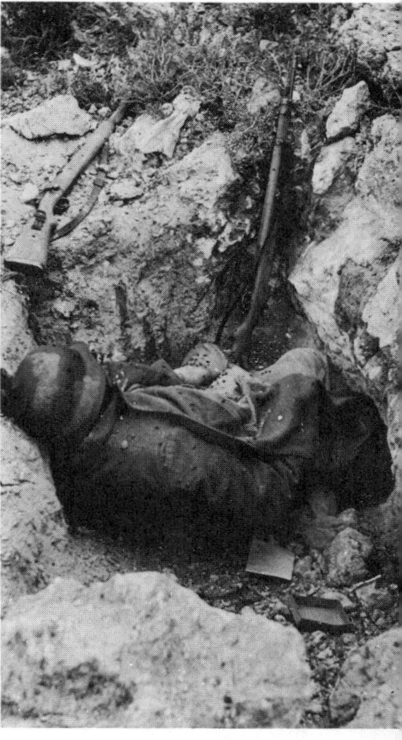

A lonely end: a dead German in his fox-hole.

Assault on Gustav Line

Friday 12 May 1944

Allied Headquarters announces: The regrouping of the allied armies in Italy has now been successfully completed without enemy interference.

The operations have been covered by continual air action and patrol activity along the whole front. Complicated and heavy road and rail movements of men and material have been smoothly carried out. This has made heavy calls on all administrative services. All formations have been involved. In spite of bad weather and difficult terrain the regrouping has been accomplished on time.

The Fifth and Eighth Armies, directed by General Alexander and supported by the Mediterranean Allied Tactical Air Force, began an attack against the Gustav Line at 11 pm on Thursday.

Increasing Violence of the Fighting in Southern Italy

Sunday 14 May 1944

German Supreme Command announces: In the Nettuno beach-head there is only a little local fighting. The fighting on the Italian southern front increased in violence, especially in the area north of Castelforte and south of Cassino. Our troops defended themselves with exemplary bravery, inflicting heavy casualties on the enemy and taking numerous prisoners. After fierce fighting and supported by massed artillery, tanks and fighter-bombers, the enemy succeeded in gaining ground in one sector. The battle continues.

Tank Clashes in the Liri Valley

Sunday 14 May 1944

Reuters *reports:* French troops of the Fifth Army have cut the Cassino-Mamurrano lateral road at one point in the Liri valley, where tank clashes have occured. Indian troops who occupied Sant'Angelo yesterday have further broken into the Gustav Line. Against bitter rearguard actions they are pushing towards high ground directly menacing the town of Pignataro, about 2½ miles beyond Sant'Angelo.

Polish Advance Halted

Tuesday 16 May 1944
The Times *reports:* Just north of the confluence of the Rapido and the Liri the bridgehead over the former river has been extended to a depth of 2000 yards by British troops. Generally speaking, however, it is clear that the operation has been so far less satisfactory north of the Liri than south of it. It will be noted that our Special Correspondent at Allied Headquarters states that the Poles, fighting on the heights north-west of Cassino, are for the moment stuck.

The long haul uphill carrying supplies to the CEF. Festooned with machine-gun belts and with boxes of grenades and cartridges, the weary troops had to carry their ammunition for miles along difficult mountain paths.

Italian Troops at the Front

Naples, 17 May 1944
Marshal Messe, Italian Chief-of-Staff, has delivered a message to the Italian soldiers who are fighting shoulder to shoulder with the Allies under the name of the 'Italian Liberation Corps'. This is the first official Italian indication that Italian troops are taking part in the offensive against the Gustav Line.

Liri Valley Flooded

Wednesday 17 May 1944
The Times *reports:* British troops fighting their way forward through the meadows of the Liri valley have found themselves opposed chiefly by 75mm. assault guns and tanks. The broad valley bottom, which undulates slightly is dotted with small farms and is cut up by small streams and gulleys which favour a dispersed defence. The water-courses make effective tank obstacles, and as well the Germans have flooded the fields where possible, so advance is bound to be slow.

Bitter Struggle on 35km Front in Southern Italy; Immense Battle of *Matériel*

Wednesday 17 May 1944
German Supreme Command announces: In the mountainous terrain of the Italian southern front a battle of *matériel* is raging on a front of 35km (20 miles). The continuous heavy bombardments, the massive expenditure of ammunition, the violent air attacks, the deployment of tanks as mobile artillery, the bitter struggle for every strong-point and every hill (which have often changed hands several times within a short period), give this fighting the character of the great defensive battles of the last world war. Against the enemy's superior strength, our troops have now been offering a heroic resistance for six days. The disengage-

Cassino towards the end of the battle; in the foreground the ruins of the old town; in the centre, Castle Hill (Rocca Janula) and in the background, dominating the landscape, Monte Cassino.

ments carried out in the course of the fighting are going according to plan. The extremely heavy casualties sustained by the enemy are out of all proportion to the purely tactical advantage of the ground won.

In the Nettuno beach-head yesterday, there was no fighting of any significance. However, enemy artillery fire, which has been intensifying for days, indicates an imminent large-scale attack there also.

Unsuccessful Attempts at Breakthrough

Wednesday 17 May 1944

Völkischer Beobachter *reports:* On Monday on the Italian southern front, the British and Americans continued their attacks with very strong infantry, armour, artillery and air forces, but the stubborn resistance of our troops again prevented the enemy's attempted breakthrough–especially in the Liri valley.

A Polish reconnaissance unit with a field telephone makes a cautious observation of German positions.

scarcely more than 35km (20 miles) wide, the British 8th and American 5th Armies launched an enormously powerful and determined onslaught on the German defences in this mountainous region. In spite of bad weather and difficult terrain, a comprehensive re-grouping of the Allied forces had been carried out previous to this operation. The British 8th Army was transferred to the most difficult sector–that of Cassino–while the Americans were grouped in the coastal sector and advanced to attack the Aurunci Mountains. The French under General Juin are also fighting in the 5th Army, on an exposed position on the southern slopes of the Aurunci which descend to the Liri valley. In the sector north of Cassino, by the frequently mentioned Rapido river, Polish units are fighting shoulder to shoulder with the British. An extraordinary mixture of peoples, British, Indians, French, Moroccans and other Africans, Poles and Americans, are welded together here under one centralized command and made to serve a common cause. A certain rivalry is noticeable between these differing nations; the French together with their colonial troops made an excellent showing and contributed much to the success of the enterprise.

Rome Liberated

Monday 5 June 1944
The Times *reports:* Rome has been liberated by Fifth Army tanks and infantry.

IN MID-MARCH 1944 Lt.-General Anders, together with his Chief-of-Staff, Colonel Wisniowski, met the commander of the 8th Army. Lt.-General Leese informed him that it had been decided to mount a major offensive in the spring, from the Tyrrhenian Sea as far as Monte Cassino. By capturing Monastery Hill and crossing the Rapido south of Cassino, the 8th Army, together with the strengthened US 5th Army, had the task of establishing a connection with the Anzio bridgehead as quickly as possible, thus opening the way to Rome. The Polish II Corps was entrusted with the capture of Cassino and the adjacent hills. Anders has described how he was informed of his men's role:

> 'A few days before March 23, General Leese came to my headquarters at Vinchiaturo and informed me that as the renewed attacks the Allied troops were making on Monte Cassino were being repelled by the Germans, and the Allied troops at the Anzio beach-head were in a difficult position, it had been decided to open a large offensive from Monte Cassino to the Tyrrhenian Sea. The Eighth Army had received orders to break through the Gustav Line, of which the main strongholds were the Monte Cassino ridges, and the Hitler Line, which hinged on Piedimonte. It was proposed, he said, that the Polish II Army Corps should carry out the most difficult of the initial tasks, the capturing of the Monte Cassino heights and then of Piedimonte.
>
> 'It was a great moment for me. The difficulty of the task assigned to the Corps was obvious, and, indeed, General Leese made it clear that he well

General Anders, the commander of the Polish II Corps, studies the map of Cassino. Anders and his men were entrusted with the final assault on the monastery position.

Motorized Division (Maj.-General Brosset), in addition to the 2nd Moroccan Division (Brig.-General Dody), the 4th Moroccan Mountain Division (Maj.-General Sevez) and the 3rd Algerian Division (Maj.-General de Goislard de Monsabert).

Between Cassino and the Gulf of Gaeta lay various German formations. The 1st Parachute Division (Lt.-General Heidrich) and the 44th Infantry Division, the *Hoch- und Deutschmeister* (Lt.-General Franek) were in the Cassino sector. A regiment of the 15th Panzer Grenadier Division (Maj.-General Rodt) and some detachments of the 305th Infantry Division (Lt.-General Hauck) defended the Liri valley. In the coastal sector was the 71st Infantry Division (Maj.-General Raapke), strengthened by three battalions of the 44th Infantry Division. The Aurunci Mountains were secured by the 94th Infantry Division (Maj.-General Steinmetz). Elements of the 15th Panzer Grenadier Division lying on the coast, as well as sections of the 90th Panzer Grenadier Division, formed the reserve.

On Monday 27 March 1944 the US army newspaper *Stars and Stripes* and the Canadian army newpaper *Maple Leaf* openly referred to the latest Allied offensive at Monte Cassino as a failure. Two days

Radio-operators at work near the front line. During the preparations for the final offensive, strict control of radio use was a major weapon in the Allied plans for a surprise attack.

later, on 29 March, the military critic of the *New York Herald Tribune*, Major Eliot, declared that Cassino had been a costly defeat.

On Wednesday 29 March, as the weather made any large-scale operation in the Cassino sector impossible, Field-Marshal Kesselring attempted for the third time to seize the initiative on the Anzio-Nettuno front.

On Tuesday 11 April, General Alexander flew to London to discuss plans for a new offensive with General Sir Alan Brooke, the Chief of the Imperial General Staff. On the same day Lt.-General Clark left Italy in Lt.-General Eaker's aeroplane to have talks with Roosevelt and General Marshall in the USA. Allied headquarters had meanwhile decided to start the new offensive in May 1944; at this time of the year the weather and ground conditions are almost ideal, with little rain, and the change in temperature between day and night minimal.

On Monday 17 April, 51,962 soldiers of the Polish Corps began to transfer to the Cassino sector. The plan for the fourth battle of Cassino rested on a large-scale deception – Field-Marshal Kesselring was to be made to believe that the Allies had decided to abandon any further assaults on the Gustav Line, and that the next offensive would be a new landing operation, this time north of Rome, near Civitavecchia. In this way General Alexander hoped to mislead Kesselring into assembling his reserves north of Rome.

A British machine-gun crew in action. The gun in question was the Vickers machine-gun, a reliable weapon that had been employed in the First World War and was still in use more than twenty years later.

Various measures were used to convince Kesselring of this change of direction. The shift of the 8th Army's army boundary to the Cassino front was kept strictly secret, and troop movements in the forward areas were only permitted during the night. The Polish II Corps, stationed to the rear of Monte Cassino, was instructed to keep strict radio silence; for urgent messages English wireless operators had been assigned to them. The approaches to both Polish divisional command posts had been screened by miles of camouflage.

Units already in front-line positions were kept where they were. Armoured units which were being regrouped left tanks and vehicle dummies in position. While both British divisions of XIII Corps, which were to cross the Rapido and Gari, were arriving at their assembly areas, the 78th Division was openly practising river-crossing 80km (50 miles) behind the front-line; and the 78th was regarded by the Germans as the likely spearhead of an impending offensive. Work on the numerous roads necessary for crossing the Rapido was carried on only at night and carefully camouflaged by day.

As a rule new artillery was driven up to previously camouflaged positions, and the combined artillery fire was continuously checked so that the daily shell consumption remained constant and the Germans did not notice that new batteries had been brought up as reinforcements. Wireless communication was used to strengthen German

British troops in readiness for yet another assault on German positions. In the background is an M4 Sherman tank while above the crew of a Bren gun the barrel of a 17 pdr anti-tank gun is clearly visible.

Intelligence (through intercepts) in its belief that the US 26th Division and both divisions of the Canadian I Corps were intended for a landing at Civitavecchia. At the 'embarkation area' of Salerno there was brisk activity, and at Naples harbour landings were practised in broad daylight. The US 36th (Texas) Division (Maj.-General Walker), which was not to go into action until the second phase of the offensive, had been assembled between Salerno and Naples. Here they carried out intensive practices for amphibious operations. The roads leading to the embarkation points and assembly areas had been carefully marked with notices carrying the tactical call-sign of the Canadian Corps. The Allied air forces made regular reconnaissance flights over the beaches of Civitavecchia. The German agents in Naples were supplied with appropriate false material and the partisans north of Rome were put into action.

The French Expeditionary Corps, which the German reconnaissance supposed to be in Naples, was removed unseen to the small Garigliano bridgehead. It had been reinforced by two divisions – the Moroccan 4th Mountain Division (Maj.-General Sevez), besides three Moroccan battalions which corresponded to a division – and then the 1st Motorized Division (Maj.-General Brosset) and an armoured brigade. This corps of 99,000 men had the task of capturing Monte Majo, the southern pillar of the German positions at Cassino and forcing a breakthrough over the Aurunci and Petrella massif which towered over the German Gustav Line. The plan which General Juin had submitted in January was to be realized at last.

Now the entire Expeditionary Corps, crowded together east of the Garigliano, was lying on the narrow plain of Sujo. Thanks to the innumerable smoke-pots, its camouflage was so perfect that the smoke not only concealed the concentration of a whole army on ground affording no cover, but also enabled six emergency bridges to be erected without the Germans noticing anything. The camouflage of both Canadian divisions standing beside the Rapido and Gari before Cassino was also totally successful.

Field-Marshal Kesselring actually allowed himself to be deceived by the preparations for a landing north of Rome. Two German divisons, one of which was armoured, now lay at Civitavecchia; elements of two armoured divisions stood in reserve in the Anzio-Nettuno area, ready to be transferred to Civitavecchia.

On Wednesday 19 April 1944, the Combined Chiefs-of-Staff instructed General Wilson to support Operation 'Overlord', the Allied landing in Normandy, by destroying and pinning down as many enemy forces as possible in the Mediterranean.

Until the end of April the front had remained quiet; even in the Cassino sector fighting was limited to outpost skirmishes.

On Friday 5 May Polish soldiers brought a German deserter into the command post of the 5th Kresowa Infantry Division. He claimed he was from the 7th Company of the 200th Panzer Grenadier Regiment, and described positions which stretched from the mountain massif over Piedimonte and the Liri valley, to shore up and prevent the collapse of the Gustav Line. The ancient stronghold of Piedimonte was to become another Monte Cassino. Laid out in a defensive zone 800m (875 yards) deep, the positions consisted of mine-fields, tank ditches and barbed wire entanglements as well as numerous gun turrets set into the ground, with 8.8cm guns.

The German summer defence of 1944 was formed by three lines which were to bar the way to Rome – the Gustav Line, which ran along the Rapido, the Adolf Hitler Line 9km (6 miles) behind it, built around Christmas 1943 and also known as the Senger Line, and beyond that, south of Rome, the Caesar Line. New defence works were also built further north, such as the Gothic Line, which sealed off Italy level with Florence.

The four main Allied attacks, running west to east, were to be made by the US II Corps (Maj.-General Keyes), the French Expeditionary Corps (General Juin), the British XIII Corps (Lt.-General Kirkman) and the Polish II Corps (Lt.-General Anders). Facing them were I Parachute Corps (Air Force General Schlemm) and LXXVI Panzer Corps (Panzer General Herr) at Anzio, XIV Panzer Corps (Lt.-

An observer looks out from his well camouflaged post, checking German positions with his prismatic compass.

General von Senger und Etterlin) on the Garigliano and the LI Mountain Corps (*General der Gebirstruppen* – General of Mountain Troops – Feuerstein) in the mountains.

A total of twenty-one Allied divisions and eleven units of brigade strength were facing fourteen German divisions and three units of brigade strength. While the Allied divisions each contained nine battalions, however, the German divisions had only six battalions and the armoured divisions only four Panzer grenadier battalions. The Allied units were rested and refreshed, several of them even at full strength, while the German units, with their inferior fighting strength, were already exhausted and heavily reduced. There was an unfavourable ratio of between 1 : 3 and 1 : 5 in terms of infantry; in terms of equipment and fire-power it went up to 1 : 10.

Facing the Polish II Corps was the 3rd Parachute Regiment (Colonel Heilmann). The regiment had already borne the main brunt of the fighting during the last Cassino battle. After its 3rd Battalion had been regrouped and transferred to France at the end of April 1944, it only consisted of two weak battalions. The 4th Alpine Battalion (Major von Ruffin), part of the 3rd Parachute Regiment, was defending Monte Cairo (Point 1669).

A British soldier surveys the wreckage of a German motorized column on the Via Casilina. Such columns were very vulnerable to Allied air superiority, and the movement of supplies and reinforcements in daylight could be a dangerous business.

Incidentally, the soldiers of the Polish II Corps learnt the latest news about any agreements between the Western Allies and Stalin to the detriment of Poland by means of the German propaganda transmitter *Wanda*, which broadcast a programme in Polish four times a day from Rome – two hours and fifty minutes altogether. Its most frequent message was, 'Polish soldiers! Are you aware what game you have been dragged into? In this situation we are your only escape – come over to us, and you will see your homeland again!' The propaganda was scarcely worth the effort. Only five soldiers out of 50,000 decided in favour of this 'shortest route' towards the homeland.

The most important sector held by the Polish Corps was 2km (1¼ miles) wide, and extended from the village of Cairo to Portella in the north and from the Via Casilina across the northern outskirts of Cassino to Le Pestinelle in the south. The most significant German strong points in this sector were the abbey of Monte Cassino, Colle Sant'Angelo (Point 601) and Monte Calvario (Point 593). Colle Sant'Angelo was the key position. Taking it would isolate Monte Cassino and the abbey, facilitating its capture, and establishing contact at the same time with the adjacent British XIII Corps which was fighting in the Liri valley. This strong point therefore had to be the main target of II Corps. Again, the only possible way of reaching Point 601 was to thrust into a sector – bounded on the left by the massif containing Points 593 and 569, and on the right by a ridge (Point 706) – which extended from Monte Castellone (Point 771) to Colle Sant'Angelo.

In this sector the strong points were secured by German advance lines of defence which lay along the whole length of Point 517, known as Phantom Ridge (in Polish, *Widmo*).

For six weeks the Allied Air Forces had been bombing German supply lines, in Operation 'Strangle'. Railway traffic north of Rome did almost come to a complete halt, but with the help of coastal shipping and by taking advantage of darkness, Kesselring succeeded in getting supplies to his troops.

The success of the Allied deception can be gauged by the fact that such experienced generals as von Senger und Etterlin, commanding XIV Panzer Corps, and von Vietinghoff, Commander-in-Chief of the 10th Army, as well as Lt.-General Baade, Commander of the 90th Panzer Grenadier Division went on leave shortly before the Allied offensive or were about to do so.

On Thursday 11 May it was dull and rainy, and in the afternoon fog rolled into the Rapido valley.

At 23.00 hours (according to the time-signal given by BBC London) about 1600 guns opened an intense bombardment on the German positions along the 30km (18 miles) stretch of the front from the coast to the upper Rapido valley. The Germans were carrying out reliefs that night, and were completely taken by surprise. Private B. of the 4th Alpine Battalion:

> '. . . I was on watch in front of the platoon command post. It was a still, warm evening, with only the sound of the enemy's harassing fire now and again . . . From the gully, the rattle of harness and the clatter of hooves could be heard. The pack-animal detachment of the 3rd Company had arrived. In a house by our command post someone was chopping wood . . . Steps approached the dug-out, the trench patrol on its rounds . . . the soldiers detailed to fetch meals came back . . . Suddenly, as if a light had been switched on, there was a blaze of flame down the valley . . . and then ear-splitting screaming, whizzing, exploding, banging and crashing . . . I squeezed into the narrow cover-hole. Splinters buzzed over me, stones and clods of earth whirled through the air. The ground trembled under the force of the blasts . . .'

Forty-five minutes after the firing began, the trusty mountain fighters of the 2nd Moroccan Division (Brig.-General Dody) and the Moroccan 4th Mountain Division (Maj.-General Sevez) on the right

The Allied assault along the whole front, May 1944.

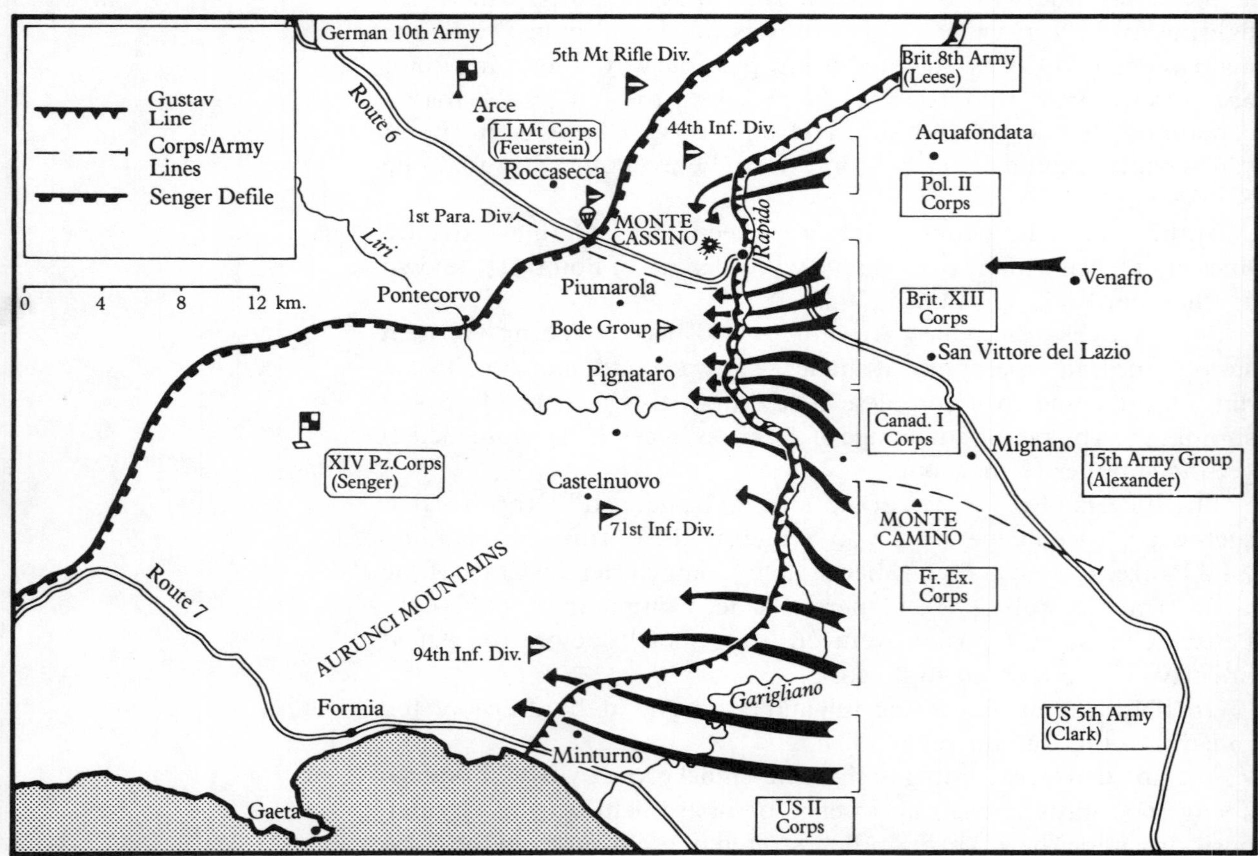

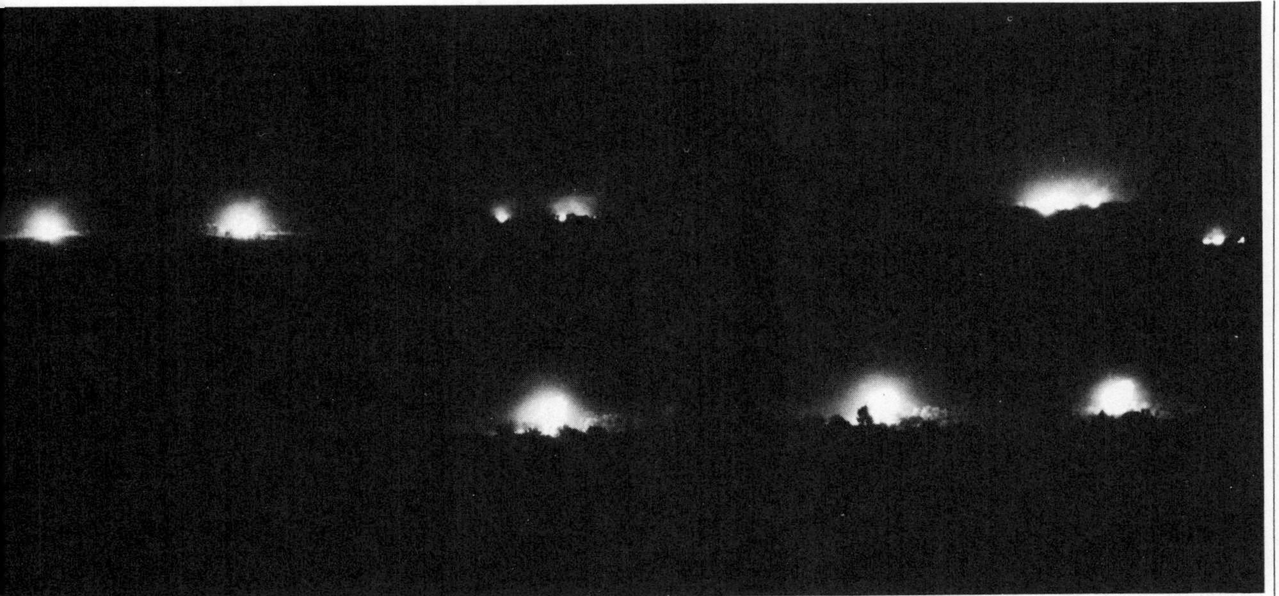

11 May, 23.00 hours: the intense Allied bombardment of the German defensive line which preceded the French assault on Monte Majo.

wing of the US II Corps (Maj.-General Keyes) attacked Monte Faito, in the middle of the Aurunci Mountains. Although the German 71st Infantry Division (Maj.-General Raapke) followed Hitler's instruction 'to fight to the last man', Monte Faito fell into the hands of the Moroccan 8th Rifle Regiment by 3.00 am on 12 May. Skilfully taking advantage of the trackless mountains, the four French divisions together drove deep into the German positions. At mid-day the Moroccan 8th Rifle Regiment took Monte Feuci, and, shortly afterwards, Monte Majo. These successes by the troops of General Juin automatically brought forward the US II Corps (Maj.-General Keyes), although in their sector the German 94th Infantry Division (Maj.-General Steinmetz) made an extremely gallant stand. The capture of Monte Majo, 900m (3000 feet) high, gave General Juin command of the heights leading along the Aurunci Mountains to the southern side of the Liri valley.

At 11.50 pm, five minutes after the French Expeditionary Corps had begun to attack, the 8th Indian and British 4th Divisions on the right wing of the French launched their assault boats into the current of the Rapido south of Cassino. In spite of intense German fire they extended their bridgeheads on the further bank.

Along a 35km (20 mile) front a total of 1600 guns, 2000 tanks and 3000 aircraft were thrown in; that is equal to forty-three guns, fifty-seven tanks and eighty-five aircraft to each 1000m (1100 yards), not counting the infantry with their weapons.

At 1.00 am, the battalions of the Polish II Corps went into the attack.

The Polish soldiers were in good heart, secure in the knowledge of their immense material superiority.

With remarkable, death-defying courage the 13th and 15th Battalions of the 5th Kresowa Infantry Division advanced to attack Point 517 (*Widmo*). They were immediately met by heavy artillery and mortar fire and suffered losses of about twenty per cent. The pace of the attack became slower and slower in the pitch darkness and the battalions reached *Widmo* almost one hour later than planned. German fire had disorganized the assault groups and contact with the brigadier had been lost. Two companies of the 13th Battalion (Colonel Kaminski) who pushed down from the north were the first to reach Phantom Ridge, but they ran into an artillery and mortar barrage, as well as machine-gun fire from the front and both flanks. Both companies also suffered considerable losses from mines and traps and were almost completely wiped out as fighting units.

Two other companies of the Polish 13th Battalion, which had reached Phantom Ridge from the south, were now under constant German fire. The 15th Battalion (Colonel Stoczkowski), advancing as part of the left wing, climbed Phantom Ridge in the darkness, and, between bushes and boulders, began to battle with the occupants of the bunkers. Two companies succeeded in passing the bunkers and reaching Point 517. Here they were caught by enemy fire and had to withdraw again. The situation of both battalions on Phantom Ridge

Soldiers of the 5th Kresowa Infantry Division lob grenades at German positions on Phantom Ridge. Among the rocks and thorn bushes, the grenade was a most effective weapon.

appeared more and more hazardous. Part of the force was overwhelmed by German counter-attacks; telephone lines were broken, radio sets destroyed and the operators killed.

The struggle for Monte Calvario (Point 593) was to become the critical issue for the 3rd Carpathian Rifle Division. The companies of the 2nd Battalion – at intervals of scarcely 100 paces – clambered up a narrow path, intending to mount as near as possible to the summit of Monte Calvario under the protection of their own artillery fire. It was a race against death. During the Allied artillery fire the Germans were forced to withdraw from their positions and strong-points into shell-proof shelters. The moment the artillery fire ceased, the soldiers ran back to their abandoned positions or took cover behind the nearest rocky outcrop, ready to fire. The Poles realized that only seconds separated them from success or failure. If they did not succeed in reaching the positions while they were still empty, they would receive the German machine-gun fire at point-blank range. On Point 593 the Poles were lucky; two platoons of the 1st Company succeeded in occupying the German positions from the east and south before the paratroopers, who were hidden in shelters, could regain them. Thanks to a lightning-quick appraisal of the situation, the Poles had reached the empty German positions together with the final artillery shells. They were thus able to overcome the defenders before they were fully prepared. In close combat, ten German artillery observers were taken prisoner. Meanwhile, the 3rd Company took Point 593 from the west, and ordered one of its platoons in the direction of Massa Albaneta. In the shelters in the rock, seventeen prisoners surrendered.

A section of Polish troops run up a gully on the slopes of Monte Cassino.

Monte Calvario was defended by the 1st Battalion of the 3rd Parachute Regiment; its 1st Company was holding the summit. Although overrun by the Carpathians several times, they put up a stiff resistance and only after stubborn close combat lasting thirty minutes was Monte Calvario finally captured by the Poles.

Four times the Germans attempted to regain Monte Calvario, using the minimal reserves of the 1st and 2nd Battalions of the 3rd Parachute Regiment, including the 7th Company, but each time they were driven back by the defenders.

The tactics of the Carpathians – so successful on Point 593 – broke down in the attack on the adjoining Point 569. Here the artillery fire ceased much too soon, so that the Germans were able to take up their positions again, unmolested, and greet the Poles with concentrated machine-gun fire. The attack came to a standstill on the saddle between the heights.

At 6.30 am the Polish 18th Battalion (Colonel Domon) reached Phantom Ridge, under the impression that most of the ridge had already been cleared of Germans. Their appearance led to an even

A British mortar detachment in action. The carefully positioned ammunition cases would give the crews some protection against German retaliatory fire.

greater concentration of Polish troops and increased the casualties caused by the growing intensity of the artillery fire.

The attack on Massa Albaneta by the 3rd Carpathian Rifle Division was supported by the Polish 2nd Armoured Brigade. While still far from their objective, the tanks were met by heavy fire from medium artillery and many of them burst into flames; others were destroyed by mines. Of twenty engineers from the mine-clearing detachment eighteen were killed or wounded. The attack on Massa Albaneta by the 15th Carpathian Brigade collapsed with heavy casualties.

By 7.15 am Maj.-General Duch, commander of the 3rd Carpathian Rifle Division, decided that in spite of considerable initial success and the capture of Point 593, the attack by II Corps had failed. He hoped to pursue it again during the coming night.

At sunrise the Allied fighter-bombers appeared over the front line. Co-operation between them and the ground troops was excellent. The machines were in radio communication with the advanced command posts. They circled constantly above the German positions and were ready to be hailed 'like a cab' to attack at once any targets specified.

Right at the beginning, the headquarters of the 10th Army (Colonel-General von Vietinghoff) in Auezzano and the command post of XIV Panzer Corps (Lt.-General von Senger und Etterlin) were knocked out after massed air attacks.

Towards mid-day the Polish garrison on Monte Calvario numbered one officer and twenty-nine men. A reserve company temporarily improved the situation. At the same time the troops, whose morale had been boosted by their obvious material superiority, began to show signs of stress.

At 19.00 hours the paratroopers made a fresh counter-attack on Monte Calvario. The 14th Company of twenty-two men, and the reserve of the 3rd Parachute Regiment, finally took possession of the mountain, and the last Polish defenders, an officer and seven men, retreated again.

Some of the troops – mainly those from the Polish 15th Battalion – remained on Phantom Ridge until dusk. On account of the enormous losses suffered General Anders felt forced to withdraw his men. The soldiers were absolutely exhausted; many of them were in a state of shock or wounded. Yet their sacrifices had not been in vain. Their action had diverted the German artillery fire and relieved their comrades of the British XIII Corps fighting in the Liri valley.

The first attack by the Polish II Corps had brought scarcely any tactical advantage and was really no more than a very costly reconnaissance. The high losses demonstrated that the simultaneous occupation of Point 593 (Monte Calvario), Point 517 (*Widmo*) and Point 601 (Colle Sant'Angelo) was necessary for success. None of these points could be held on its own. During the fighting, it had also became clear that even a platoon was too large a unit, its equipment too heavy and cumbersome, for an attack at close quarters on fortified mountain positions.

German defensive fire quickly destroyed radio and field telephone connections, and the runners brought in to transmit messages, of whom there were too few in the companies, mostly arrived too late or not at all. In a short time, therefore, the commanders lost their general view of developments in the battle-field. The situation was not helped by the fact that the messages arriving at the headquarters were imprecise and often false.

The disposition of the artillery of II Corps was also unfortunate. The light artillery stood about 7km (4½ miles), the medium about 9km (6 miles) behind the front line. The light artillery thus had to fire at maximum range, which considerably restricted accuracy and caused dispersion. Neither had any opportunity of making direct observations and fired on the basis of the inexactly mapped results of air reconnaissance. All they could do was to fire in the general direction of

General von Vietinghoff, the experienced commander of the German 10th Army, at an observation post.

the front. The divisional artillery, used to support the attacking companies, found that the steep, mountainous terrain again made close support, directional fire or protection for the infantry completely impossible.

The 3rd Carpathian Rifle Division did receive thirty-six new mortars, ideal for mountain warfare, but they arrived so late that the troops could not be trained in time. The same applied to the flame-throwers, which, besides, were too heavy and formed too good a target for snipers. Their containers exploded when hit by a small splinter or bullet, and gave no hope of escape to the three-man crew.

At Albaneta another problem was presented by the wrecks of the Allied tanks, lying abandoned since the imprudent advance over the Cavendish Road on 19 March 1944. The paratroopers had turned them into dangerous strong-points, occupied by snipers armed with rifles with telescopic sights or machine-guns which hit targets at extreme range.

The German defensive tactics were simple and effective. The paratroopers – reinforced, and in well camouflaged, scarcely discernible positions – rarely fired at long range. This was the task of the artillery, mortars and heavy machine-guns, which mainly fired from the flank. As a rule, the paratroopers let the attacker approach closely and only then mounted their counter-attacks, with every available means, in groups of only a few men – equipped with light machine-guns, sub machine-guns and hand grenades. Each small, well-disguised strong-point was prepared to fight to the last man and kept its nerve when it was cut off. The German artillery batteries demonstrated variety, versatility and mutual support. High-angle or flat trajectory blocking and flanking fire made it possible to fire rapidly and flexibly at points of main effort, as well as to form massed barrages and destroy the enemy concentrations. The network of artillery observation posts was almost perfect, although there was no artillery observation from the air. Each battery had a main observation post and an advanced observer; in addition, artillery and infantry regularly exchanged information.

The cardinal error had been General Leese's refusal to allow the Polish II Corps to reconnoitre the terrain. The heavy mortar fire, as well as the threat of snipers had even made observation of the immediate terrain impossible from the forward positions. By denying reconnaissance, Leese had (successfully) attempted to conceal the presence of the Polish Corps from the enemy, but the lack of information had particularly injurious consequences when the order came to storm the unfamiliar mountain slopes by night.

Strangely enough, observation posts were also lacking at divisional and brigade level. The Corps received 4000 camouflage nets, 7000 camouflage uniforms and a million sandbags. Each division had an engineer battalion, and there was also a corps engineer battalion, yet even the construction of observation posts for the ten artillery regiments was omitted.

The Corps had been positioned in the sector assigned to it for almost three weeks, but the plan of action was drawn up in the rear areas using aerial photographs, staff maps annotated by aerial photograph interpreters, plastic scale models, and on the basis of experience gained in the first three battles. The fact that the mountainous terrain and the excellent camouflage made it impossible for aerial photographs to pick up the most important German positions, and that the ones detected were often only dummies, was ignored.

In the evening of 12 May 1944 General Alexander judged the result of the first day of the new battle to be unsatisfactory. In the 8th Army sector, the Polish Corps had had to withdraw its attacking troops to their initial positions, and the British XIII Corps had not attained half of the objectives which were to have been reached in the first two hours. The US II Corps could not even break through the fortified German positions in its sector.

In fact, on the first day of the fourth battle of Cassino only General Juin was able to report a decisive success. In its rapid advance, his

An infantry mortar attempts to give effective support to an Allied attack. Yet against the well sited German positions, the Allies expended a vast amount of ammunition with only limited success.

Expeditionary Corps had already broken the right wing of the German LI Mountain Corps (General of Mountain Troops Feurstein). General Alexander, who perceived a possible opportunity here, now ordered the Canadian I Corps (Lt.-General Burns) to push towards Pontecorvo.

The violent fighting south of Cassino in the Liri valley went on for the entire night of 12/13 May. Further bridges were built over the Rapido, and the bridgeheads expanded slightly.

Almost half of the battalions of the Polish II Corps which had been thrown into action were unfit for battle for the next few days. The troops required a comprehensive reorganization, and Lt.-General Leese informed General Anders that II Corps was not to attack until the complementary encirclement of Cassino town by the 8th Indian and British 4th Divisions from the Liri valley had made definite progress towards its objective.

On Saturday 13 May 1944, Field-Marshal Kesselring hurled his available reserves against Leese's 8th Army in order to delay the fall of Cassino. He wanted to gain time for his threatened units to withdraw and occupy a second line of defence, the Adolf Hitler Line (also known as the Senger Line).

Out of the independent Moroccan supply battalions, the goumiers (soldiers of the warlike mountain races of North Africa) and a regiment

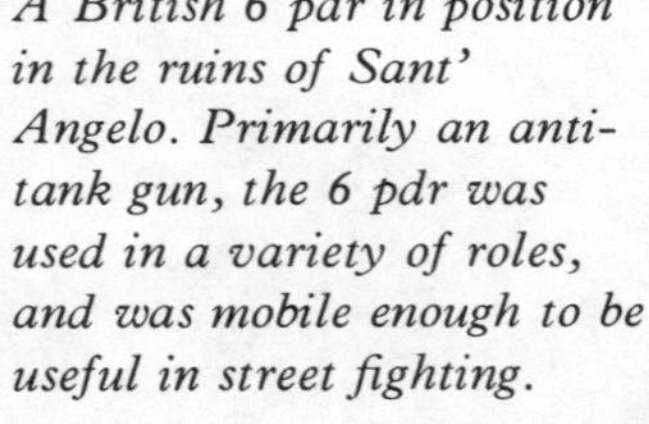

A British 6 pdr in position in the ruins of Sant' Angelo. Primarily an anti-tank gun, the 6 pdr was used in a variety of roles, and was mobile enough to be useful in street fighting.

of the Moroccan 4th Mountain Division, General Juin now put together a mountain assault force totalling 12,000 men and 4000 mules. While the Moroccan Rifle Division and the mountain troops were fighting the German rearguards in the mountains, the French 1st Motorized Division pressed on with all speed, taking Santa Andrea in the evening, and the 1st Moroccan Infantry Division reached the Liri.

The US II Corps (Maj.-General Keyes) was meanwhile making painful progress, as the divisions recently arrived from the USA had not yet had enough experience of battle. Supported by heavy naval artillery, they were ordered to force a breakthrough on both sides of the Via Appia, overcome the enemy in the southern sector of the Senger Line and join up with the troops in the Anzio beach-head.

On Sunday 14 May, the 1st Moroccan Infantry Division thrust forward to San Giorgio on the right bank of the Liri. On the right wing of the French Expeditionary Corps the 3rd Algerian Infantry Division captured Castelforte. Now the way was clear for the mountain assault force set up the day before. Using mule-tracks, the goumiers climbed the rugged chain of the Aurunci with their pack-animals, meeting hardly any German resistance. The German High Command had not thought it possible that the Aurunci Mountains could be crossed by troops, and for long the Allied commanders had been of the same opinion. This assault force now captured Monte Rotondo, overran the 15th Panzer Grenadier Division (Maj.-General Rodt) and reached the Ausente valley.

Thus, forty hours after the opening of the fourth battle, the southern hinge of the Cassino position had been forced – not through the efforts of the mighty Allied motorized units and over 3000 aircraft, but through the persistence of the North African infantryman, the individualistic fighter from the Atlas Mountains. Without him, the new Allied offensive would perhaps also have failed. But now the great victory was at hand.

While the Poles were suffering the severest casualties on Monte Cassino and the British XIII Corps (Lt.-General Kirkman) was only gradually expanding its bridgeheads on the Rapido, the defenders of the Cassino sector were being increasingly threatened by the French from the south.

In this phase of the battle General Juin decided the fate of Monte Cassino on the Garigliano. As he had already wanted to do before the first battle of Cassino in January 1944, his troops now attacked the Via Casilina through the Aurunci Mountains from the south instead of assaulting the defences on the Cassino gap and the surrounding mountains. In this way he achieved the penetration and consequent breach of the previously impregnable Gustav Line, and broke the German ability to resist. The Moroccan 4th Mountain Division now

French troops crewing a Bofors anti-aircraft gun. Despite the strength of the Allied air forces there remained the constant threat of surprise German air raids which could wreak havoc in the crowded Allied rear areas.

The gaunt remains of the Benedictine Abbey of Monte Cassino. Now a strongpoint for the German paratroops, it remained a focal point of the battle, and not until the whole line was outflanked could the Allies force the Germans out.

prepared their surprise attack deep into the Gustav Line, across the 1533m (5000 feet) high Monte Petrella massif.

In the south on the other hand, the US II Corps in the coastal sector was only able to take Santa Maria Infante after heavy fighting.

Just as serious was the plight of the British XIII Corps on the Rapido. British engineers in the 4th Division's sector did not succeed in throwing a pontoon bridge over the Rapido until 8.00 am on 14 May. A little later the British took Sant'Angelo, and in order to seal off Cassino and Monastery Hill, the famous British 78th Division (Maj.-General Keightley) was also sent into action.

Field-Marshal Kesselring now threw all his available reserves (including those he had been holding in readiness for a landing north of Rome) into the Cassino area.

During the night of 14 May, the goumiers from the mountain assault force climbed Monte Fammera, north of Spigno.

In the early morning the British 78th Division was ordered by XIII Corps to cross the Rapido, break out of the bridgehead and after a wheeling movement outflank Cassino from the valley. After a short, heavy bombardment by twenty-one artillery regiments, XIII Corps went into the attack, and slowly and painfully, the 4th Division gained ground. The 1st Parachute Machine-Gun Battalion, although almost totally obliterated, nevertheless offered such fierce resistance that a breakthrough in the direction of Cassino could not be achieved. During the night of 15 May, the 8th Indian Division in the Cassino sector took the town of Pignataro after a short fight.

At the same time the French captured the key German positions on a slope above Ausonia, which extended into the Liri valley at right-angles, and during the day they captured Monte Petrella and Monte Revole.

On Tuesday 16 May, after a ten-minute preliminary bombardment, a company from the 16th Battalion (Major Stańczyk) of the 5th Kresowa Infanty Division stormed Phantom Ridge in order to make a reconnaissance. They succeeded in taking and holding some German positions, and, in order to exploit this success, Major Stanczyk had two further companies attack; during the night of 16 May the whole northern section of Phantom Ridge fell into Polish hands. By sunrise on 17 May, the Polish 15th Battalion (Colonel Stoczkowski) had captured the southern slope of Phantom Ridge, and so, on the morning of 17 May, the Polish II Corps made a fresh attack. This time, too, Colle Sant'Angelo and Monte Calvario (Point 593) were the main targets.

Right at the beginning, the 5th Kresowa Infantry Division penetrated deep into the German positions on Colle Sant'Angelo and Phantom Ridge. But a fierce immediate counter-attack by the 1st Parachute Division threw back the Poles, who suffered extremely heavy casualties. Meanwhile, down in the Liri valley, an attempt by the British 4th Division to capture Cassino town had also failed.

May 1944: British troops on the slopes of Rocca Janula prepare to move forward under cover of mortar fire.

By the afternoon of 17 May, the goumiers had the Aurunci Mountains behind them and were standing on the Itro-Pico road, about 40km (25 miles) to the rear of the German Cassino front. Shortly afterwards they were on the Via Casilina; and this drive by General Juin's men brought about the fall of Monte Cassino. Now too, the British 78th Division fought its way through to the Via Casilina and advanced north towards Rome.

The last pillars of the German front-line defences, Cassino and Monastery Hill, the scene of such fierce fighting for so many months, had lost all importance, for the German 10th Army under von Vietinghoff was threatened with being surrounded from the south. Field-Marshal Kesselring now prepared to order the 1st Parachute Division to retire. Sections of this formation had been almost completely wiped out – the 1st Company of the 1st Battalion of the 3rd Parachute Regiment, for example, consisted of just one officer, one NCO and one soldier.

The US II Corps also began to make better progress on the coast and captured Formia on the same day.

Soldiers of the Scots Guards securing the ruins of Cassino with the Castle Hill rising up in the background. The Scots Guards were acting in a supporting role for the Polish II Corps who were assaulting the monastery from Phantom Ridge.

At 18.05 hours, the official war diarist of the Polish II Corps noted, 'Commanding General of II Corps informs the Commander of the 3rd Carpathian Rifle Division of the possibility that the enemy might retreat from Cassino during the night. Cassino station is being bombed by German aircraft during the night.'

At 23.30 hours the official log of II Corps recorded, 'Some enemy aircraft circled above the corps sector and dropped flares. Bomb explosions were heard from the direction of Cassino.' The attack on Cassino station was the agreed signal for the staff of the 1st Parachute Division to retreat from the Cassino sector.

The fact that the commanders of the Polish II Corps had known hours beforehand of the impending German retreat and the air attack on the station, was entirely owing to the 'Ultra Secret'. The most important sources of information for the Allies were the German radio messages themselves, which the British Secret Service, thanks to the construction of a German encoding machine, 'Enigma', had been able to read since 1940. This enterprise had a long history. In Warsaw in 1932, a team of three young Polish mathematicians, J. Rozycki, M. Rejewski and J. Zygalski, succeeded in deciphering the code of the German coding machine, 'Enigma', through an intensive study of

A German soldier in the ruins of the abbey. The buildings were now mere shells of their former selves, but portions of the immensely strong stonework still remained.

cycle theory. And some months before the German invasion of Poland, in the summer of 1939, these three scholars pulled off a great coup – they constructed an imitation 'Enigma'. On hearing this news, Major G. Bertrand, head of the relevant section of the French Secret Service, travelled to Warsaw on 24 July 1939. The British experts, Commander Denniston and the mathematician Knox, were also on the spot. And two days later they received possibly the most precious gift presented by Poland to her allies before the outbreak of war: two imitation German coding machines. One of them remained in Paris, the other went to London and was initially received there with great scepticism.

In the autumn of 1939, cryptographers from the Secret Intelligence Service (SIS) set up their headquarters in Bletchley Park, a country house north of London. An ancestor of the present-day computer was installed to help decode enciphered messages transmitted by 'Enigma' and then intercepted. At the head of this most secret of all British operations (Codename 'Ultra') was Wing Commander F. W. Winterbotham, who was responsible at the same time for handing on the decoded 'Enigma' messages to Churchill.

Thus, all orders given by German Supreme Command (operational

A photograph taken at 10.00 am on the morning of 18 May: 2nd Lieutenant Gurbiel's patrol. On the left is Sergeant Wroblewski and Gurbiel himself is standing third from the left.

intentions; unit strengths and positions; the composition of attacking forces) and other important secret intelligence came into the hands of General Alexander's staff often no later than the addressees received it.

Wing Commander Winterbotham: 'I suppose, looking back on it, that 'Ultra' during the Italian Campaign had given us almost as complete a picture of the German side as could have been found in Kesselring's files in his office in Rome . . .'

General Alexander: 'The knowledge not only of the enemy's precise strength and disposition but also how, when and where he intends to carry out his operations has brought a new dimension into the prosecution of the war.'

Towards midnight the last paratroopers abandoned their positions on Monte Cassino without a fight, and under cover of darkness struggled through the mountains to the next line of defence, the Senger Line, near Piedimonte. During the night of 17/18 May 1944, patrols in the sector of the 3rd Carpathian Rifle Division found indications that the Germans had also abandoned Monastery Hill.

At dawn, the 4th Battalion made a renewed attack on Point 493 and eventually captured it about 7.00 am. As there was no more firing from Monastery Hill, Maj.-General Duch, Commander of the 3rd Carpathian Rifle Division, ordered the 12th Podolski Lancer Regiment to reconnoitre. About 8.00 am, the 4th Platoon of the 1st Squadron from the Divisional Reconnaissance Regiment sent out a patrol of thirteen men under Lieutenant Gurbiel towards the abbey. The patrol made their way rapidly but carefully through the boulders of the ravaged mine-fields. Between Points 450 and 445, a mine-field about 300m (320 yards) wide and 100m (110 yards) deep barred the approach to the monastery 300m (320 yards) below the abbey.

At the foot of Monastery Hill Gurbiel left six men on guard with a machine-gun, and himself went with six men to the monastery ruins. Now that the previously impregnable fortress was before their eyes, they seemed to forget the danger lurking at every step. Gurbiel:

> '. . . A thick haze, mixed with the morning mist, rolled up the valley. The sun, appearing over the mountains, was like a tarnished golden ball. The stink of decay hung over the hill, and the light breeze made it even more unbearable. Only the shimmering, blood-red poppy-fields, defying the shells and bombs, waved softly in the wind . . .'

After they reached the mighty ruined walls, which from below towered up to the sky, Sergeant Wadas climbed on to Sergeant-Major Wroblewski's shoulders. He pulled himself up on to the walls and was the first to enter the abbey. A few minutes later he returned and reported that no-one was to be seen. At a sign from Lieutenant Gurbiel, all of them scaled the walls at 9.45 am.

Silently they clambered over heaps of rubble and found sixteen wounded soldiers there, with two medical orderlies and an ensign. Gurbiel:

> 'It was clear that the enemy soldier was first-rate and highly disciplined. We spoke German to the prisoners. The ensign requested fifteen minutes' time to get himself ready. I of course agreed. I collected the prisoners, who could all walk, with the exception of three or four wounded, and sent them to the squadron.'

In the nearby dungeons, Gurbiel's men discovered enough tinned food to feed a whole regiment. At 9.50 am, Lieutenant Gurbiel stuck up a branch, displaying a 12th Podolski Lancer Regiment's pennant hastily cobbled together from parts of a Red Cross flag and a blue handkerchief, on the ruined walls. Shortly afterwards, section-leader Czech played the Kraków *Hejnal* (a medieval Polish military signal) on the bugle. Section-leader Choma:

> 'There was a lump in my throat as, through the echo of the cannon's roar, the notes of the *Hejnal* rang out from the abbey . . . These soldiers, hardened by numerous battles, only too well acquainted with the shocking wastefulness of death on the slopes of Monte Cassino, cried like children, as, after years of wandering, they heard not from the radio, but from the previously invincible German fortress, the voice of Poland, the melody of the *Hejnal* . . .'

The Battle of Monte Cassino was at an end.

Section-leader Czech, on Monte Cassino on 18 May 1944.

EPILOGUE

Opposite: The aftermath of battle, burying the dead.

It was at once tragic and fitting that it should have been the Poles who finally, without a shot being fired, captured the fiercely contested monastery of Monte Cassino.

The Polish soldiers – more than any other of the Allied troops who fought for months around Monastery Hill – felt a particularly deep and permanent connection to this holy place, where they had suffered such heavy losses and whence, 1000 years before, the Catholic faith and Christian culture had been carried to their homeland after the birth of the Polish state.

Meanwhile the fighting raged on elsewhere. When the Allies forced their way out of the Anzio-Nettuno bridgehead on Tuesday 23 May 1944, the badly mauled 14th Army under von Mackensen, had to fall back. On 25 May, while the Poles occupied Piedimonte, thus breaking into the Senger Line at long last, Maj.-General Truscott's troops captured the town of Cisterna. The beach-head units of the US 5th Army had at last broken out of their encirclement. In spite of this the Germans gave the Americans a tactically skilful running fight: defiant rearguard actions frequently halted the Allied advances, and the withdrawal never degenerated into flight.

Kesselring, deceived by the original Allied plan, tried desperately to retrieve the situation, but he had scarcely any reserves. The advance units of the US 5th Army were already near Valmontone and preparing to cut off the German 10th Army's escape route to the north, inflicting thereby a crushing defeat.

On the afternoon of 25 May, however, Maj.-General Truscott was surprised to receive an order from Lt.-General Clark to alter the direction of his main drive north-west away from Valmontone, and press on directly to Rome. Truscott confessed himself bewildered, but

German prisoners are escorted back from the ruins of the town of Cassino past a Sherman tank by cheerful Allied soldiers.

the publicity-seeking Lt.-General Clark nurtured the suspicion that the British had prepared plans to be the first to arrive in the Eternal City, and Clark was determined to go down in history as the conqueror of Rome. Later he wrote that he probably over-reacted to signs that his allies wanted to forestall him. But before the last battle for Cassino began, General Alexander had made it quite clear that none other than the US 5th Army should capture Rome.

Ultimately, this change of direction by Mark Clark worked to the advantage of the sorely-pressed Kesselring. A substantial part of the 10th Army succeeding in escaping from the trap which Maj.-General Truscott had wanted to set at Valmontone.

On Sunday 4 June 1944, while the last rearguards of the German 4th Parachute Division were evacuating the northern districts of Rome without a fight, units of the US 88th Division were beginning to occupy the town, and they were astonished to find that none of the many bridges over the Tiber had been destroyed. This had been done on Kesselring's express orders. He was mindful of the military disadvantage, but had decided to protect the Eternal City from destruction.

On the following morning, Monday 5 June, Clark celebrated the capture of Rome with a press conference on the Capitoline Hill.

There now followed a relentless pursuit, and Field-Marshal Kesselring could easily have been driven out of Italy. The invasion which had taken place in Normandy on 6 June 1944 was developing successfully, and nothing seemed to stand in the way of a crushing Allied victory in Italy which, in accordance with Churchill's far-sighted and urgent wish, would lead them towards central Europe. But nothing of the sort was to happen.

When General Marshall, Chief of the US General Staff, came to Rome, Wilson, Alexander and others entreated him to push on at the appropriate moment across the Adriatic, through the Croatian littoral, the Ljubljana basin and Hungary, up to Vienna. He categorically

American Rangers go over the top as they break out of the German stranglehold. These were the elite troops of the US Army, the equivalent of the British Commandos.

refused, however, deciding, in agreement with General Eisenhower, in favour of Operation 'Dragoon', the invasion of the South of France. At the climax of a victorious pursuit, the US 5th Army had to provide seven of its best divisions for this operation.

At first Kesselring took this to be a subtle move in the game; but when what he scarcely dared to hope proved to be true, he was able to return to his trusty delaying tactics with renewed vigour. Hence, at the end of the summer of 1944, the weakened Allied troops were faced with another fortified mountain barrier, this time the Gothic Line south of the Po, and were held there from August 1944 until the Allied breakthrough in April 1945.

On 15 August 1944, in response to Stalin's urging in Teheran a year before, the Allies landed on the Côte d'Azur. This offensive had little point, however. Apart from the garrisons of Toulon and Marseille, Hitler immediately pulled all his troops out of southern and south-western France. There was thus no prospect of encircling large German units or influencing in any way the operations in northern France. Lt.-General Clark:

The combined breakthrough to Rome.

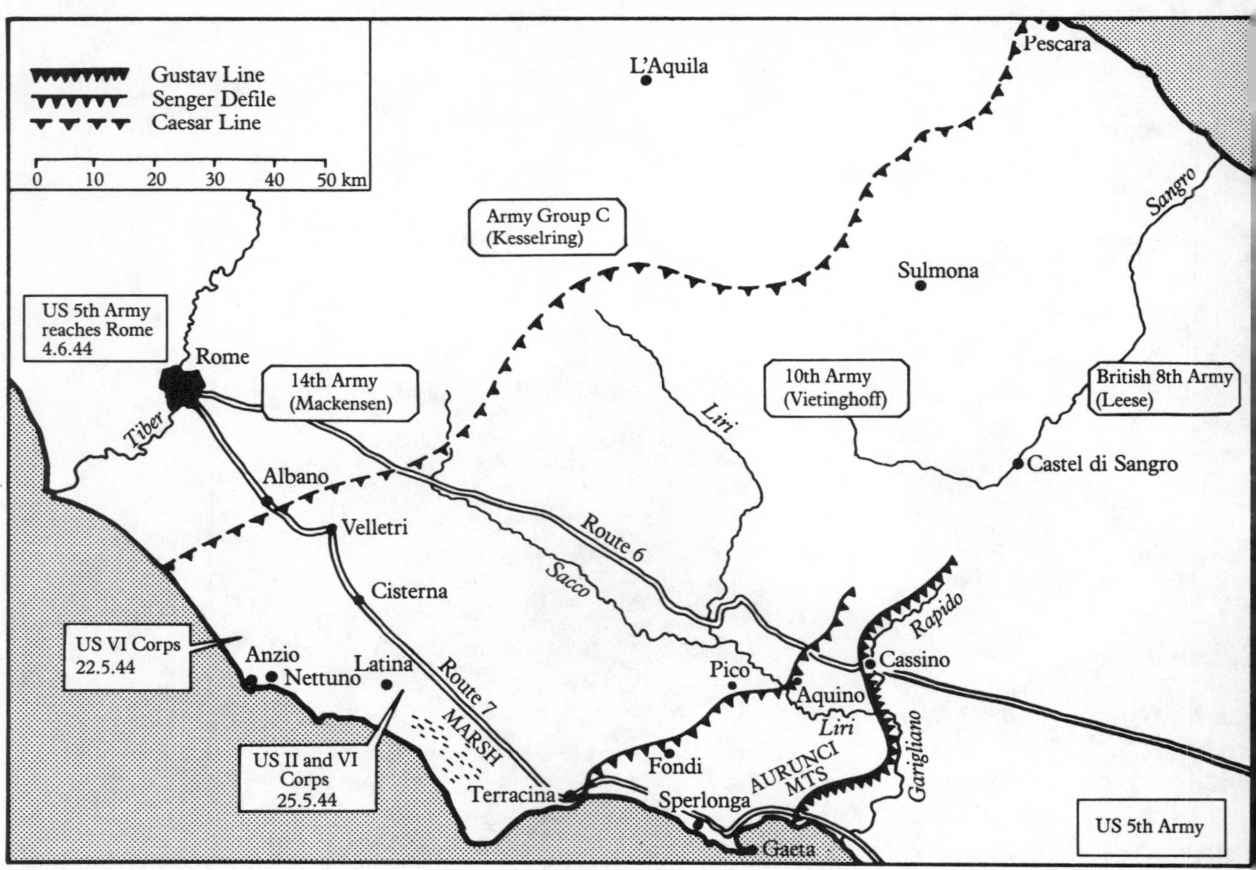

Mark Clark in Rome, June 1944.

'As it turned out, the men, material and air forces needed for "Anvil" simply stripped the 5th Army of its strength . . . I believe that there is plenty of evidence from other sources to support my attitude. For instance, there was Marshal Kesselring, whose intelligence section was completely mystified in coming weeks when our great forward drive failed to take full advantage of its chance to destroy the beaten and disorganized German Army in Italy. . . . The Russian point of view I also consider most interesting. Stalin, it was evident, throughout the Big Three meetings and negotiations at Teheran was one of the strongest boosters of the invasion of southern France. He knew exactly what he wanted in a political as well as a military way; and the thing he wanted most was to keep us out of the Balkans . . .'

In this way the war in the Mediterranean theatre and Italy was reduced to a sideshow, and in spite of all the efforts and hopes of Churchill and Alexander, the Battle of Monte Cassino remained only an episode, a mountain war in its harshest form – with about 350,000 wounded, dead and missing on both sides – which the British General J.F.C. Fuller rightly called, 'tactically the most absurd and strategically the most senseless Campaign of the whole war'.

BIBLIOGRAPHY

Alexander, H. R.: *The Allied Armies in Italy from 3rd September to 12th December 1944, London Gazette*, 12 June 1950

Anders, A. W.: *An Army in Exile*, London 1949

Bieganski, S.: *Działania 2. Korpusu we Włoszech*, London 1963

Bielatowicz, J.: *3. Batalion Strzelców Karpackich*, London 1949

Blumenson, M.: *Bloody River*, London 1970

Blumenson, M.: *Anzio, the Gamble that failed*, London 1963, New York 1963

Böhmler, R.: *Monte Cassino*, Darmstadt 1955

Bryant, A.: *Triumph in the West – The War Diaries of Field Marshal Viscount Alanbrooke*, London 1959, New York 1959

Buckley, C.: *Road to Rome*, London 1945

Burdon, R. M.: *History of the 28th Battalion*, War History Branch of the New Zealand Government, Wellington 1953

Butler, J. R.: *History of the Second World War, Vol. II*, HMSO, London 1957

Carpentier, M.: *Forces Alliées en Italie*, Paris 1949

Chambe, R.: *Le Bataillon du Belvedere*, Paris 1956

Churchill, S. W.: *The Second World War, Vol. V, Closing the Ring*, New York 1951, London 1952

Clark, W. M.: *Calculated Risk*, New York 1950

Cody, J. F.: *History of the 21st Battalion*, War History Branch of the New Zealand Government, Wellington 1953

Cody, J. F.: *History of the 28th (Maori) Battalion*, War History Branch of the New Zealand Government, Wellington 1956

Connell, C.: *Monte Cassino – The Historical Battle*, London 1963

Davis, M.: *Who Defends Rome?* London 1972

De Gaulle, C.: *Mémoires de Guerre*, Paris 1956

Ehrman, J.: *History of the Second World War, Vol. V*, HMSO, London 1957

Eisenhower, D. D.: *The Papers of D. D. Eisenhower, Vols I–V*, Baltimore/London 1970

Fuller, J. F. C.: *The Second World War 1939–1945*, London 1948

Harris, C. R. S.: *Allied Military Administration of Italy*, HMSO, London 1957

Higgins, T.: *The Soft Underbelly*, London 1957

Hoppe, H.: *Die 278. Inf.Div. in Italien*, Bad Nauheim 1953

Juin, A.: *La campagne d'Italie*, Paris 1962

Kesselring, A.: *Soldat bis zum letzten Tag*, Bonn 1953

Kippenberger, H.: *Infantry Brigadier*, London 1961

La Distruzione di Monte Cassino: Documenti e Testimonianze, Monte Cassino 1950

Leccisotti, T.: *Montecassino*, Badia di Montecassino 1971

Le Goyet, P.: *La participation Française et la Campagne d'Italie*, Paris 1969

Liddell-Hart, B.: *History of the Second World War*, London 1972, New York 1972

Linklater, E.: *The Campaign in Italy*, London 1951

Majdalany, F.: *Cassino*, London 1957

Martin, T. A.: *The Essex Regiment 1929–1950*, Brentwood 1952

Martineau, G. D.: *A History of the Royal Sussex Regiment*, Chichester, n.d.

Młotek, M.: *Trzecia Dywizja Strzelców Karpackich 1942–1947*, London 1978

Mordal, J.: *Cassino*, Paris 1952

Nicholson, G. W. L.: *The Canadians in Italy 1943–45*, Official History, Ottawa 1957

North, J.: *The Alexander Memoirs 1940–1945*, London 1962

Orgill, D.: *The Gothic Line*, London 1967

Pal, D.: *The Campaign in Italy, Official History of the Indian Armed Forces in the Second World War 1939–1945*, India & Pakistan 1960

Phillips, N. C.: *New Zealand in the Second World War, Official History: Italy, The Sangro to Cassino*, War History Branch of the New Zealand Government, Wellington 1957

Piatkowski, H.: *Bitwa o Monte Cassino*, Rzym 1945
Pringle, J. C./Clue, W. A.: *History of the 20th Battalion and Armoured Regiment*, War History Branch of the New Zealand Government, Wellington 1957
Puttick, E.: *History of the 25th Battalion*, War History Branch of the New Zealand Government, Wellington 1960
Ray, C.: *Algiers to Austria, A History of 78th Division in the Second World War*, London 1952
Schimak, A./Lamprecht, K./Dettmer, F.: *Die 44. Infanterie Division*, Vienna 1969
Shepperd, G. A.: *The Italian Campaign 1943–1945*, London 1968
Sinclair, D. W.: *History of the 19th Battalion and Armoured Regiment*, War History Branch of the New Zealand Government, Wellington 1954
Smith, E. D.: *The Battles for Cassino*, London 1975
Starr, G. C.: *From Salerno to the Alps, A History of the Fifth Army 1943–1945*, Washington 1948
Stevens, G. R.: *Fourth Indian Division*, Toronto 1956
Truscott, L. K.: *Command Missions*, New York 1954
Tuker, F.: *Approach to Battle*, London 1963
Wagner, L. R.: *The Texas Army*, Austin 1972
Walker, L. F.: *From Texas to Rome*, Dallas 1969
Wańkowicz, M.: *Bitwa of Monte Cassino*, Milan 1945
Westphal, S.: *The German Army in the West*, London 1951
Wilmot, C.: *The Struggle for Europe*, London 1957
Wilson, H. M.: *Report by the Supreme Allied Commander, Mediterranean, to the Combined Chiefs of Staffs on the Italian Campaign, Part I*, HMSO, London 1946

Periodicals and documents

American Rifleman, The, May 1944; *Cassino Close-up*, by B. Shadel
Bacque, P.: *Carnet de Route, 8 Janvier – 4 Février 1944*
Berge – Flüsse – Inseln, *Geschichte und Geschichten der Insel-Division und Italiens (90. Pz.Gren.Div.) o.J.*
Das Kleeblatt, Nachrichtenblatt der 71. Infanterie-Division, 1944 *Der Reichsgrenadier*, 1944
Die Südfront, 1944
Eighth Army News, Fourth Indian Division by F. Redman. August 29, 1944
Gebirgsjäger-Rgt. 100 (5. Geb. Div.) in den Cassino-Schlachten, by A. Glasl, National Archives, Washington D.C. 1946
Le Mistral, Bulletin des Officers de Réserve de Marseille. XXXIV. Année, No. 259, 1961
Saturday Evening Post, The, 18 May 1946; *They'll Never Forget Mark Clark*, by S. Feder.
Time, 28 January 1946; *Murder at the Rapido?*
Under Hail of Fire, Iowans enter Cassino, by H. Boyle, 1947
United States Government Printing Office, *The Rapido River Crossing*. Hearings before the US Congress House, Committee on Military Affairs, House of Representatives, 79th Congress, Second Session. Washington D.C. 1946
Von Senger und Etterlin, F.R.T.: *War Diary of the Italian Campaign, Cassino*. Historical Division Headquarters US Army, Europe, National Archives, Washington D.C. 1947
Warlimont, W.: *The Drive on Rome*, Historical Division European Command, National Archives, Washington D.C. 1947
Von Vietinghoff, H.: *The Operations of the 71st German Infantry Division during the month of May 1944*, National Archives, Washington D.C. 1946
XIII Corps Intelligence Summary No. 450, Appendix B, National Archives, Washington D.C. 1944
XIV Panzerkorps, Taktische Meldungen, National Archives, Washington D.C. 1946
44. Infanterie-Division, Mitteilungsblatt der Kameradschaft, Vienna 1965

INDEX

Figures in italics refer to captions

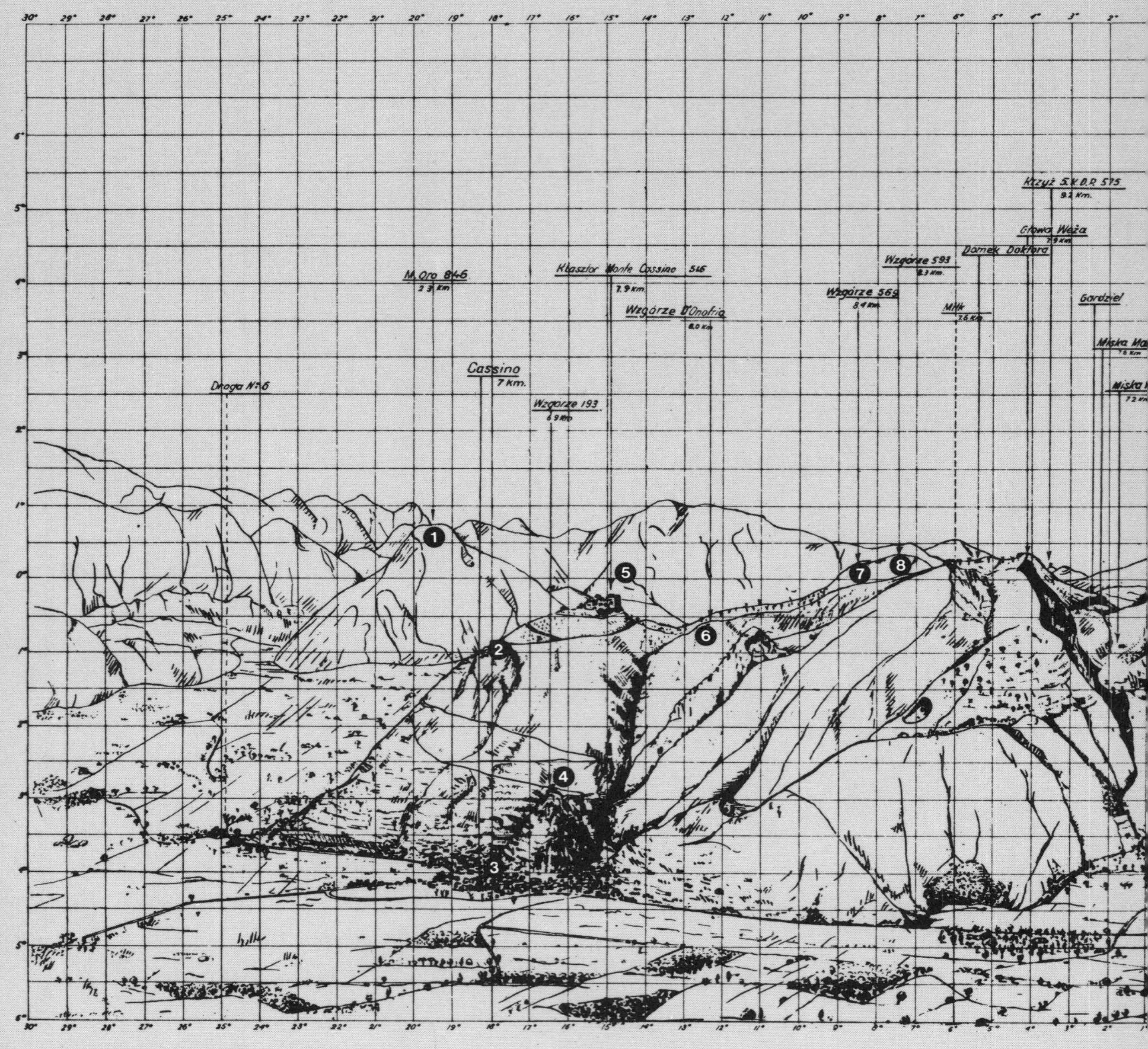

A Polish map of the Cassino sector, looking across the Rapido valley from the Allied side. This map was used by the artillery of the Polish Corps.